Refresher Vocabulary & Grammar Tests for Advanced Proficiency Exams

RICARDO MADUREIRA

Refresher Vocabulary & Grammar Tests for Advanced Proficiency Exams

With answers

3ª Reimpressão

DISAL
EDITORA

Preparação de texto: Larissa Lino Barbosa / Verba Editorial
Capa e Projeto gráfico: Alberto Mateus
Diagramação: Crayon Editorial
Assistente editorial: Aline Naomi Sassaki

Dados Internacionais de Catalogação na Publicação (CIP)
(Câmara Brasileira do Livro, SP, Brasil)

Rodrigues, Ricardo Madureira
Refresher vocabulary & grammar tests for advanced proficiency exams : with answers / Ricardo Madureira Rodrigues. -- Barueri, SP : DISAL, 2014.

Bibliografia.
ISBN 978-85-7844-165-4

1. Inglês - Atividades, exercícios etc. 2. Inglês - Estudo e ensino 3. Inglês - Gramática 4. Inglês - Provas e exames 5. Vocabulário - Estudo e ensino I. Título.

14-06791 CDD-420.7

Índices para catálogo sistemático:
1. Inglês : Estudo e ensino 420.7

DISAL EDITORA

Alameda Mamoré 911 - cj. 107
Alphaville - BARUERI - SP
CEP: 06454-040
Tel. / Fax: (11) 4195-2811
Visite nosso site: www.disaleditora.com.br
Televendas: (11) 3226-3111

Fax gratuito: 0800 7707 105/106
E-mail para pedidos: comercialdisal@disal.com.br

Summary

Letter to candidates

Dear reader,

If you intend to sign up for an advanced proficiency examination, such as Cambridge CAE/CPE (British English, University of Cambridge, England) or Michigan ECPE (American English, University of Michigan, EUA), it is advisable to do a thorough review , as these tests are highly demanding.

This book focuses on vocabulary and grammar, two central aspects of the exams. These sections appear clearly divided in the Michigan ECPE, and the multiple-choice tests in this book will give you an idea of what the official exam questions look like. Cambridge exams test grammar and vocabulary interwoven in all sections, that is, you are not tested separately on any one specific item, as is the case for Michigan ECPE.

The vocabulary review in this book consists of 50 units with 10 vocabulary items each, providing you with a wealth of synonyms and definitions. These synonyms are especially useful for the Brazilian learner, because they are basically Latin words, which we recognize more promptly. We would advise you to carefully check for the effective use of Latin words in a good monolingual dictionary, as they may be inadequate in everyday, informal language.

I hope you enjoy studying this book, as much as I have enjoyed writing it.

Moreover, remember, "The only place where success comes before work is in the dictionary!"

Best wishes,
Ricardo

Lessons Structure Overview

This book consists of 50 lessons with the following structure:

Stage 1 Vocabulary is presented in 10 sentences. The word studied is highlighted in boldface and italics. Read the sentences and try to figure out the meaning of the word or expression. If the sentence level context does not allow you to make a guess, it might be useful to look the word up in a dictionary.

Stage 2 Synonyms and definitions are presented from A – J, so you can match them with the words 1 – 10 from stage 1. Latin cognates are usually shown as the last option, so that the readers can familiarize themselves with the more current words. (All the units follow the same structure.)

Exam Practice Each cycle of five units concludes with Exam Practice exercises, with twenty multiple-choice grammar tests (Michigan ECCE/ ECPE format), plus ten "Key Word Transformation" tests, replicating the format of Cambridge examinations. Answers to all the questions are provided in the key at the end of each five unit cycle. As this is a review book, explanations in the key are brief and straight to the point.

Rounding Off As a way of concluding each cycle of every five units, this is a section in which the words studied are recapitulated and consolidated through review . It consists of two parts: the first one deals with reviewing meanings, while part two is concerned with affixes (word formation table).

Answer Key This is provided at the end of every cycle of five units.

Extras 10 extra sections at the end of the book are presented to boost your vocabulary: ① *true friends* ② *false friends* ③ *idiomatic verb + noun collocations* ④ *idiomatic prepositional phrases* ⑤ *idiomatic adverbial phrases* ⑥ *phrases with similar structure but different meanings* ⑦ *idiomatic uses of* *common nouns and adjectives* ⑧*phrasal verbs* ⑨*phrasal verb related nouns* and ⑩*make* or *do? (special collocations)*

Vocabulary Booster, Final Review The book is rounded off with a vocabulary booster test containing 200 hundred multiple-choice questions followed by key.

Foreword

I believe learning a new language, especially a language such as English, which is used internationally, means gaining entry into a new world of possibilities, which reminds me of this moving poem engraved on the pedestal where the Statue of Liberty, one of the world's most famous landmarks, stands.

May English be to you, as the poem says, "the lamp beside the golden door" in your studies and aspirations.

The New Colossus

EMMA LAZARUS*

Not like the brazen giant of Greek fame,
With conquering limbs astride from land to land;
Here at our sea-washed, sunset gates shall stand
A mighty woman with a torch, whose flame
Is the imprisoned lightning, and her name
Mother of Exiles. From her beacon-hand
Glows worldwide welcome; her mild eyes command
The air-bridged harbor that twin cities frame.
"Keep ancient lands, your storied pomp!" cries she
With silent lips. "Give me your tired, your poor,
Your huddled masses yearning to breathe free,
The wretched refuse of your teeming shore.
Send these, the homeless, tempest-tost to me,
I lift my lamp beside the golden door!"

(*) **Note**: Emma Lazarus (1849 - 1887) was born in New York. She descended from the Jewish. In this poem, she pays homage to the cherished idea that the United States was a country which welcomed people from all over the world seeking work, asylum, freedom and justice. This ideal might have been blurred by the more recent facts in history, but the idea of the United States as a welcoming country is still prevalent among many people.

10 MINUTES A DAY

LESSON 1

Stage 1 Read the sentences carefully and try to figure out the meaning of the word or expression in bold from the context. Then, go on to the next Stage.

1 The Native Americans tried to ***appease*** their gods' wrath by making offerings to them.
2 There are books which are only intended for the ***discerning*** readers.
3 I hate it when politicians appear on TV with their ***hackneyed*** slogans.
4 No one ***owned up*** to the stealing of the company's money.
5 I know you're having a hard time, but don't ***take it out on*** me. It's not my fault.
6 I've had a ***hectic*** routine lately. I've been working hard every single day.
7 Don't worry about accommodation. I'll ***put you up*** for the night.
8 The candidate is, ***by all accounts***, a very respectable and competent man.
9 The soldiers faced a dreadful ***ordeal*** when they had to attack the enemy.
10 We could smell the wonderful scent of her perfume ***lingering*** in the room.

Stage 2 Match the words and expressions with their definitions or synonyms:

a) ___ [ADJECTIVE]: unoriginal, trite, commonplace, clichéd
b) ___ [NOUN]: painful, trying experience
c) ___ [VERB]: pacify, placate
d) ___ [ADJECTIVE]: busy, hushed
e) ___ [ADJECTIVE]: showing a good sense of judgment about art and culture
f) ___ [NOUN]: according to the widely accepted view
g) ___ [VERB]: admit, confess
h) ___ [VERB]: remaining for a long time
i) ___ [VERB]: treat someone badly because you are angry
j) ___ [VERB]: allow someone to stay in your house temporarily

10 MINUTES A DAY

LESSON 2

Stage 1 Read the sentences carefully and try to figure out the meaning of the word or expression in bold from the context. Then, go on to the next Stage.

1 He was a man of ***altruistic*** feelings towards humanity.
2 Even though I didn't agree at first, I had to ***acquiesce*** to the plan in the end.
3 You won't find the word in this compact dictionary. You'll need a ***comprehensive*** version.
4 Because of your ***foolhardy*** behavior, you're always getting yourself into trouble.
5 Would severe punishment really act as a ***deterrent*** to bullying in schools?
6 Authorities are trying to ***do away with*** capital punishment in this country.
7 If you wish to live longer, you'll have to ***cut down on*** smoking.
8 His behavior at school has improved ***appreciably***, but his grades still need improving.
9 There were so many ***casualties*** in the accident that it caused widespread shock.
10 My father was a ***callous***, heartless man, who was unable to show compassion.

Stage 2 Match the words and expressions with their definitions or synonyms:

a) ___ [ADJECTIVE]: reckless, not worrying about consequences of actions
b) ___ [NOUN]: something which acts as an obstacle, impediment
c) ___ [NOUN]: dead or injured victims
d) ___ [VERB]: reduce the amount of
e) ___ [VERB]: agree, give in reluctantly
f) ___ [ADJECTIVE]: unfeeling, insensitive
g) ___ [ADJECTIVE]: unselfish, philanthropic
h) ___ [ADJECTIVE]: complete, unabridged
i) ___ [VERB]: abolish, ban
j) ___ [ADVERB]: considerably, significantly

10 MINUTES A DAY

LESSON 3

Stage 1 Read the sentences carefully and try to figure out the meaning of the word or expression in bold from the context. Then, go on to the next Stage.

1 He hopes everyone will recognize his ***unsung*** merits one day.
2 I do not ***condone*** any kind of violent punishment in this school.
3 Given the circumstances, I felt ***compelled*** to help.
4 There were a lot of ***rabid*** religious leaders in the procession.
5 Her ***outgoing*** personality earned her a lot of friends.
6 Don't ***miss out on*** good opportunities in life.
7 The writer was a complete success, but he had such an ***unassuming character***.
8 Education has do deal with ***illiteracy*** urgently if it is to improve in this country.
9 He expressed his ***unreserved*** admiration for the writer's new novel.
10 My teacher asserted her authority with ***unrelenting*** rudeness.

Stage 2 Match the words and expressions with their definitions or synonyms:

a) ___ **[ADJECTIVE]**: fanatical
b) ___ **[NOUN]**: inability to read
c) ___ **[ADJECTIVE]**: never ceasing, untiring, relentless
d) ___ **[ADJECTIVE]**: extrovert
e) ___ **[ADJECTIVE]**: unknown, unrecognized
f) ___ **[VERB]**: agree (especially with negative things)
g) ___ **[ADJECTIVE]**: shy, modest
h) ___ **[ADJECTIVE]**: open, complete, without any doubt
i) ___ **[VERB]**: forced, coerced
j) ___ **[VERB]**: lose out

10 MINUTES A DAY

LESSON 4

Stage 1 Read the sentences carefully and try to figure out the meaning of the word or expression in bold from the context. Then, go on to the next Stage.

1 There were ***scathing*** remarks about the principal's decision.
2 Her appearance was ***hideous*** after spending the whole night drinking.
3 The ***heinous*** murders shocked the quiet neighborhood.
4 His talent was ***overshadowed*** by his much more gifted brother.
5 She was a ***loathsome*** woman who didn't respect anyone.
6 Teachers lose respect when they ***go back on*** their word.
7 The students tried to leave the classroom ***unobtrusively*** so as not to be noticed by the teacher.
8 Everyone felt ***downtrodden*** by the authoritarian boss's rude remarks.
9 The movie was ***overrated*** in my opinion. It's not as good as it was advertised.
10 His ***delusional*** behavior kept everyone away from him.

Stage 2 Match the words and expressions with their definitions or synonyms:

a) ___ [ADJECTIVE]: being treated disrespectfully by people who have power over you
b) ___ [VERB]: to make feel less important (figuratively: cast a shadow over)
c) ___ [VERB]: give up doing something you've promised to do
d) ___ [ADJECTIVE]: have a belief that you are more important than you really are
e) ___ [ADVERB]: in a way that you are not noticed easily
f) ___ [ADJECTIVE]: severe, caustic criticism about something
g) ___ [ADJECTIVE]: shocking, terrifying
h) ___ [ADJECTIVE]: repulsive
i) ___ [ADJECTIVE]: extremely ugly, unpleasant
j) ___ [ADJECTIVE]: give something more importance than it really deserves

10 MINUTES A DAY

LESSON 5

Stage 1 Read the sentences carefully and try to figure out the meaning of the word or expression in bold from the context. Then, go on to the next Stage.

1 He was feeling lost in a ***maelstrom*** of confusing emotions.
2 This is ***arguably*** one of the most important scientific breakthroughs of the century.
3 You can ***tackle*** this problem in many different ways.
4 There was a ***staggering*** number of people in the concert.
5 There's a ***glaring*** mistake in your conceptions.
6 Our plans to travel ***fell through*** when we took a look at the weather forecast.
7 The excellent food in the hotel ***makes up for*** the staff's unfriendliness.
8 I like the countryside, but there are some ***drawbacks*** to living here.
9 Too much internet use is ***detrimental*** to your concentration on your studies.
10 The cell phone is now a ***ubiquitous*** possession. Everybody wants one.

Stage 2 Match the words and expressions with their definitions or synonyms:

a) ___ [ADJECTIVE]: obvious, easily noticed
b) ___ [VERB]: deal with, attack
c) ___ [ADJECTIVE]: having a damaging effect on something
d) ___ [NOUN]: disadvantage, inconvenience
e) ___ [NOUN]: turmoil, agitation
f) ___ [ADVERB]: possibly
g) ___ [ADJECTIVE]: found everywhere, omnipresent, universal
h) ___ [VERB]: compensate for
i) ___ [ADJECTIVE]: astounding, astonishing, mind-boggling
j) ___ [VERB]: fail to happen

EXAM PRACTICE 1
GRAMMAR

Part 1 Multiple-choice

1 I was to ____ traveled, but my car broke down on the weekend.

a) have

b) be

c) had

d) been

2 If it ______ not been for her help, I wouldn't be a professional now.

a) were

b) did

c) was

d) had

3 No sooner had he left, ______ the rain started.

a) so
b) then
c) when
d) than

4 I had to study _________ for the exam.

a) hardly
b) hard
c) much
d) very

5 I traveled on vacation, _________ the forecast of unfavorable weather.

a) although
b) even though
c) in spite
d) despite

6 _____ for my teacher's guidance, I wouldn't have been able to finish the end term paper.

a) Not
b) Due
c) But
d) Despite

7 Outsourcing is the process _______ which a company employs workers from outside the company.

a) with
b) by
c) for
d) at

8 I'd rather you ________ say anything about what happened.
a) wouldn't
b) hadn't
c) didn't
d) shouldn't

9 The teacher would prefer to walk to school rather than ______ by bus.
a) to go
b) going
c) gone
d) go

10 "I have a sore throat."
"Why don't you try ________ some tea?"
a) to drink
b) drinking
c) drink
d) drank

11 This is the first time I ________ this movie.
a) have seen
b) see
c) am seeing
d) saw

12 __________ thought to be lots of people working illegally in the United States.
a) They are
b) It is
c) Many are
d) There are

13 "I can't speak a foreign language. What about you?"
"I can't __________".

a) either
b) neither
c) too
d) also

14 You haven't forgotten it's my birthday, _________?

a) isn't it
b) did you
c) have you
d) haven't you

15 I am always arriving late for class, __________?

a) am I not
b) isn't it
c) don't I
d) aren't I

16 This movie is so boring. We _________ as well go home.

a) can
b) may
c) should
d) will

17 Try as I ________, I didn't get a good grade in math.

a) may
b) did
c) could
d) might

18 The workers were ________ injured in the accident.

a) deadly
b) dead

c) fatally
d) clean

19 Have you got ________ information you need?
a) all the
b) every
c) many
d) an

20 Paul behaves _____________ he were a child.
a) although
b) as though
c) though
d) as like

Part 2 Key Word Transformation

Rewrite the second sentence so that it has a similar meaning to the first sentence, using the word given. Do not change the word given. Use between two and eight words, including the word given. An example has been done to help you.

EXAMPLE: If you had worked harder, you would have money now. **(only)**
If only you had worked harder, you would have money now.

1 You cannot leave the classroom without my permission. **(unless)**
You cannot ___________________________.

2 I would have failed the exam if John had not helped me. **(but)**
___________________________. I would've failed the exam.

3 I had scarcely sat down when I heard a knock on the door. **(than)**
Scarcely ___________________________ I heard a knock on the door.

4 I would appreciate it if you didn't tell anyone about this. **(rather)**
___________________________ anyone about this.

5 Burglars have broken into their house. **(been)**
Their house ___________________________.

6 Everyone believes that the world is coming to an end. **(widely)**
It ___________________________ that the world is coming to an end.

7 If only you weren't so obsessed. **(wish)**
I ___________________________ so obsessed.

8 It is rumored that he has been sent to prison. **(have)**
He ___________________________ prison.

9 In addition to being an excellent singer, he is an extraordinary dancer. **(apart)**
___________________________, he is an extraordinary dancer.

10 I might have been able to help you, if you had asked me. **(only)**
___________________________, I might have been able to help you.

ROUND OFF 1

1 Match the columns to find the synonyms:

1. condone	6. callous
2. rabid	7. unassuming
3. appease	8. downtrodden
4. hectic	9. staggering
5. foolhardy	10. ubiquitous

a) ___ put up with, accept, tolerate
b) ___ imprudent, reckless
c) ___ intolerant, fanatical, obsessed
d) ___ unpretentious, timid, modest
e) ___ omnipresent, pervasive, universal
f) ___ heartless, unfeeling, insensitive
g) ___ overwhelming, astonishing, astounding
h) ___ quell, placate, pacify
i) ___ busy, eventful, strenuous
j) ___ oppressed, abused, afflicted

2 Try to remember some collocations by completing the gaps with words from the units:

a) feel __________ to help
b) a __________ reader
c) a __________ possession
d) __________ to concentration
e) leave a place as __________ as possible
f) __________ aroma
g) a __________ encyclopedia

3 EXPRESSIONS – Match the columns:

1) I can't **put up with** your feeble excuses any more.
2) The Ministry of Education said racism is to be **done away with** in schools.
3) You'd better **cut down on** your daily sugar consumption.
4) If parents always **go back on** their words, children will learn to fool them.
5) My plans to sit the exam **fell through** because I couldn't study as hard as I had planned.
6) He worked hard to **make up for** his lack of experience in the field.

a) ___ put an end to
b) ___ fail, come to nothing
c) ___ endure, tolerate
d) ___ reduce
e) ___ compensate
f) ___ fail to keep a promise

4 Fill in the gaps to form a collocation pattern. Use one of these words (the meaning of the words is given in parentheses):

hackneyed	*scathing*
unsung	*heinous*
outgoing	*hideous*
unreserved	*glaring*
overrated	*unrelenting*

a) __________ support (= complete)
b) an ____________ hero (= not praised)
c) __________ sayings (= clichéd)
d) __________ remarks (= severely critical)
e) a __________ omission (= conspicuous, obvious)
f) an __________ type of person (= socially confident)
g) an __________ film (= higher than deserved)
h) ____________ crimes (= wicked, odious)
i) look ____________ hideous (= ugly, disgusting)
j) ____________ opponent (= ruthless)

5 WORD FORMATION – Complete the table with the forms which are missing. If one of the forms doesn't exist, leave the space blank:

NOUN	VERB	ADJECTIVE	ADVERB
		discerning	
	acquiesce		
		deterrent	
		comprehensive	
illiteracy			
			(un) obtrusively
		detrimental	
		ubiquitous	
	compel		
	linger		

Key to lessons 1 - 5

LESSON 1 – a) 3 b) 9 c) 1 d) 6 e) 2 f) 8 g) 4 h) 10 i) 5 j) 7
LESSON 2 – a) 4 b) 5 c) 9 d) 7 e) 2 f) 10 g) 1 h) 3 i) 6 j) 8
LESSON 3 – a) 4 b) 8 c) 10) d) 5 e) 1 f) 2 g) 7 h) 9 i) 3 j) 6
LESSON 4 – a) 8 b) 4 c) 6 d) 10 e) 7 f) 1 g) 3 h) 5 i) 2 j) 9
LESSON 5 – a) 5 b) 3 c) 9 d) 8 e) 1 f) 2 g) 10 h) 7 i) 4 j) 6

EXAM PRACTICE 1

PART I

1 A) (= "I would have traveled...")
2 D) (= "If she hadn't helped me...")
3 D) The phrase "No sooner had...," is followed by a clause introduced by "than".
4 B) Be careful: there is an important difference between "hard" and "hardly". In this case, only "hard" is possible.
5 D) "Although" and "even though" would only be possible if followed by a subject: "I traveled on vacation, even though / although <u>the weather forecast</u> was unfavorable." "In spite" would be adequate if followed by a preposition: "In spite <u>of</u> the unfavorable weather forecast, I traveled..."
6 C)) (= "If it had not been for my teacher's guidance, I wouldn't...")
7 B) (or: "... is the process <u>whereby</u> a company employs...")
8 C) (= "I'd prefer it if you <u>didn't say</u> anything...")
9 D) The grammar pattern is "would prefer" + infinitive with "to" ... "rather than" + bare infinitive.
10 B) When "try" is used to make a suggestion (and not to express an order), it is followed by the gerund.
11 A) The phrase "This is the first/second time..." is followed by the "present perfect". "This is the first time I see / am seeing this movie..." are <u>not</u> possible.
12 D) (= "It is thought that <u>there are lots of people</u> living...")
13 A) In additions to remarks in a negative statement, we use "either" or "neither". As the verb form "can't" is already in the negative, we use "either".
14 C) Question tags keep the auxiliary from the main clause ("... You <u>haven't</u> forgotten..."). Since the auxiliary is used in the affirmative form, the tag takes the verb in the negative.
15 D) Strange as it may seem, the first person takes the form "are" in question tags.
16 B) (= "Since there isn't anything better to do, let's go home.")
17 D) (= "No matter how hard I tried, I didn't...")
18 C) Collocation pattern

19 A) "Information" is an uncountable noun. "Every" is followed by singular countable nouns; "many" is followed by countable nouns in the plural; "an" cannot be followed by an uncountable noun.

20 B) (= "Paul isn't a child, but he behaves as a child does.")

PART II

1 ***leave the classroom unless you have my permission***

2 ***But for John's help***

3 ***had I sat down than***

4 ***I'd rather you didn't tell***

5 ***has been broken into***

6 ***is widely believed***

7 ***wish you weren't***

8 ***is rumored to have been sent to***

9 ***apart from being an excellent singer***

10 ***If only you had asked me***

ROUNDING OFF 1

1 a) 1 b) 5 c) 2 d) 7 e) 10 f) 6 g) 9 h) 3 i) 4 j) 8

2 a) feel ***compelled*** to help
b) a ***discerning*** reader
c) a ***ubiquitous*** possession
d) ***detrimental*** to concentration
e) leave a place as ***unobtrusively*** as possible
f) ***lingering*** aroma
g) a ***comprehensive*** encyclopedia

3 a) 2 b) 5 c) 1 d) 3 e) 6 f) 4

4 a) unreserved b) unsung c) hackneyed d) scathing e) glaring f) outgoing
g) overrated h) heinous i) hideous j) unrelenting

5

NOUN	VERB	ADJECTIVE	ADVERB
discernment	discern	***discerning***	discerningly
acquiescence	***acquiesce***	acquiescent	acquiescently
deterrence	deter	***deterrent***	x
comprehensiveness	comprehend	***comprehensive***	comprehensively
illiteracy	x	illiterate	x
obtrusion	obtrude	obtrusive	***(un) obtrusively***
detriment	x	***detrimental***	detrimentally
ubiquity	x	***ubiquitous***	ubiquitously
x	***compel***	compelling	compellingly
x	***linger***	lingering	lingeringly

10 MINUTES A DAY

LESSON 6

Stage 1 Read the sentences carefully and try to figure out the meaning of the word or expression in bold from the context. Then, go on to the next Stage.

1 The singer had a ***penchant*** for strange clothes.
2 The document was ***thoroughly*** checked for inconsistencies.
3 My enthusiasm ***wears off*** easily when I'm working with uncooperative partners.
4 She seemed ***boastful*** because she was always talking about her own qualities.
5 Drug consumption has had one of the most ***pervasive*** influences on young people.
6 The chief executive had an ***unerring*** eye for spotting a talented worker.
7 My mother was a woman with ***parochial*** attitudes , unwilling to change her points of view.
8 The new worker received the news of his promotion with ***elation***.
9 Sour milk ***gives off*** a nasty, offensive smell.
10 I was so ***engrossed*** in the song, I didn't realize the class had already finished.

Stage 2 Match the words and expressions with their definitions or synonyms:

a) ___ [ADJECTIVE]: enraptured, absorbed
b) ___ [VERB]: cease to exist
c) ___ [ADJECTIVE]: always correct, unfailing, making no mistake
d) ___ [NOUN]: great happiness, excitement, delight
e) ___ [NOUN]: a liking for something
f) ___ [ADVERB]: examine exhaustively, in detail
g) ___ [ADJECTIVE]: bragging, conceited
h) ___ [ADJECTIVE]: spread throughout
i) ___ [VERB]: emit
j) ___ [ADJECTIVE]: provincial, narrow minded

10 MINUTES A DAY

LESSON 7

Stage 1 Read the sentences carefully and try to figure out the meaning of the word or expression in bold from the context. Then, go on to the next Stage.

1 His ***disreputable*** life was a problem for him during the electoral campaign.
2 The student is making efforts in ***pursuit*** of his academic achievements.
3 It is necessary to take measures to ***ensure*** the safety of all the procedures.
4 His views on religion and politics are completely ***biased***.
5 They used to support our views, but are now ferocious ***dissenters***.
6 The boss tended to be so ***lukewarm*** towards his employees.
7 At the ***outset*** of the crisis, all the countries were fighting against poverty.
8 The motorists quarreled, both ***seething*** with rage.
9 Her ***unflattering style*** made her feel so self-conscious and inadequate.
10 The famous rock singer sang with ***panache*** and energy.

Stage 2 Match the words and expressions with their definitions or synonyms:

a) ___ [ADJECTIVE]: unattractive, ugly
b) ___ [VERB]: to make sure that something happens
c) ___ [ADJECTIVE]: not respectable, untrustworthy
d) ___ [NOUN]: beginning, start
e) ___ [NOUN]: flair, confidence
f) ___ [NOUN]: those who disagree with the general policy
g) ___ [ADJECTIVE]: unenthusiastic
h) ___ [NOUN]: quest, search
i) ___ [ADJECTIVE]: prejudiced
j) ___ [ADJECTIVE]: very angry, fuming over something

10 MINUTES A DAY

LESSON 8

Stage 1 Read the sentences carefully and try to figure out the meaning of the word or expression in bold from the context. Then, go on to the next Stage.

1 I wish you would stop ***pussyfooting*** around and say what you really think.

2 A mob of ***unruly*** demonstrators marched along the street, causing problems to the traffic.

3 He was a ***mischievous*** student, but deep inside he was a good guy.

4 Some advertisements encourage children to ***pester*** their parents.

5 The boss was angry with the worker because he had only paid ***cursory*** attention to the job.

6 "These feelings are very difficult to ***gauge***," said the psychologist.

7 His ***parsimonious*** spending habits earned him a funny nickname.

8 The new student didn't get along with the others. She was ***aloof*** and reserved.

9 The company is beginning to ***thrive*** after a critical period.

10 The committee has decided to ***put off*** the exam until a later date.

Stage 2 Match the words and expressions with their definitions or synonyms:

a) ___ [VERB]: dodge, evade, prevaricate

b) ___ [ADJECTIVE]: hasty, superficial

c) ___ [ADJECTIVE]: withdrawn, indifferent

d) ___ [VERB]: badger, vex, annoy

e) ___ [VERB]: postpone, change

f) ___ [ADJECTIVE]: mean, stingy

g) ___ [ADJECTIVE]: badly behaved, disorderly

h) ___ [ADJECTIVE]: naughty, playful

i) ___ [VERB]: prosper, make progress

j) ___ [VERB]: assess, evaluate

10 MINUTES A DAY

LESSON 9

Stage 1 Read the sentences carefully and try to figure out the meaning of the word or expression in bold from the context. Then, go on to the next Stage.

1 There have been some ***inconsequential*** changes to the plan.
2 The parents were arrested accused of ***neglecting*** their children.
3 The employment market is ***saturated*** with poorly qualified professionals.
4 There is ***widespread*** rumor about her resignation as the company's chief executive.
5 The vocabulary in this book is sometimes ***baffling*** to the average reader.
6 This medicine will ***boost*** your memory and physical energy.
7 After the destruction caused by the rain, it was necessary to build more ***dwellings*** for the poor.
8 ***Hazardous*** drinking habits have led him to develop a cancer.
9 The ***grisly*** murders shocked the locals who lived peacefully in the village.
10 Today there are songs which are popular only because of their ***risqué*** language.

Stage 2 Match the words and expressions with their definitions or synonyms:

a) ___ [VERB]: overlook, ignore
b) ___ [NOUN]: houses
c) ___ [ADJECTIVE]: dangerous, risky
d) ___ [VERB]: foster, enhance, improve
e) ___ [ADJECTIVE]: unimportant, insignificant
f) ___ [ADJECTIVE]: completely filled with something
g) ___ [ADJECTIVE]: bewildering, puzzling
h) ___ [ADJECTIVE]: common over a wide area or among many people
i) ___ [ADJECTIVE]: shocking
j) ___ [ADJECTIVE]: referring to sex in a slightly shocking language

10 MINUTES A DAY

LESSON 10

Stage 1 Read the sentences carefully and try to figure out the meaning of the word or expression in bold from the context. Then, go on to the next Stage.

1 The city of Los Angeles has become ***notorious*** for its high criminal rates.
2 There are many ***perils*** in exposing yourself on various websites.
3 We are ***on the verge of*** a sexual revolution, or so it seems.
4 Due to the heavy rain, these roads are now ***impassable***.
5 Many criminals sell drugs in the ***vicinity*** of the school.
6 Cars aren't sold at ***affordable*** prices in some countries.
7 The novel ***depicts*** the drudgery of everyday life in medieval times.
8 His handwriting is completely ***illegible***, that's why he was disqualified.
9 Advertising is thought to have dangerous ***subliminal*** messages.
10 He's a tough principal who always states his opinions ***assertively***.

Stage 2 Match the words and expressions with their definitions or synonyms:

a) ___ [ADJECTIVE]: sold at a reasonable price
b) ___ [ADJECTIVE]: places where you cannot pass because of bad condition
c) ___ [NOUN]: neighborhood, surrounding area
d) ___ [ADJECTIVE]: enjoying a bad reputation, infamous
e) ___ [VERB]: portray, represent
f) ___ [ADVERB]: said in a forceful, authoritative way
g) ___ [NOUN]: jeopardy, risks, dangers
h) ___ [NOUN]: near
i) ___ [ADJECTIVE]: which cannot be read, unreadable
j) ___ [ADJECTIVE]: below the level of conscious awareness

EXAM PRACTICE 2
GRAMMAR

Part 1 Multiple-choice

1 I had no alternative ___ to resign.

a) other than
b) but
c) unless
d) whether

2 The teacher was not sure as to ___ she would punish him or not

a) if
b) how
c) when
d) whether

3 I would have appreciated it if you ___ for your inconvenience.
a) will apologize
b) would apologize
c) had apologized
d) would had apologized

4 ___ a wonderful singer, but also a talented actress.
a) Not only she is
b) Not only is she
c) Even though she is
d) In spite of being

5 The English Language, ___ is spoken in the United States, is used as a foreign and second language in many other countries.
a) which
b) that
c) whom
d) of which

6 If you ___ sit down, the principal will talk to you presently.
a) may
b) might
c) can
d) will

7 I'll forgive you, even though ___ a conscientious student.
a) you have not always been
b) not always you have been
c) you not always have been
d) you always not have been

8 This is the man ___ daughter has been accused of drug trafficking.
a) his
b) which

c) her
d) whose

9 I haven't ___ you for such a long time! Where have you been?
a) been seeing
b) seen
c) seeing
d) been seen

10 ___, it is the people who are punished when politicians are corrupt.
a) Ultimate
b) Ultimately
c) The ultimate
d) At the ultimate

11 I have been a teacher ___ I can remember.
a) since as long as
b) since long as
c) for long as
d) for as long as

12 A microscope ___ scientists to observe invisible microorganisms.
a) makes it possible for
b) makes it possible that
c) makes possible for
d) makes possible that

13 This study ___ light on this obscure subject.
a) aims throwing
b) aims at throwing
c) whose aim throws
d) aims to throw

14 Rarely ___ such wonderful renditions.

a) I have heard
b) have I heard
c) had I hear
d) I had hear

15 Those ___ for the exam should attend a crash course review.

a) that signs up
b) signing up
c) whom sign up
d) are signing up

16 It gets real cold here ___ the winter.

a) by
b) on
c) at
d) in

17 I couldn't make ___ to the party because I was ill.

a) me
b) you
c) it
d) go

18 Sorry about what I've done. I'll make it up ___ you somehow.

a) for
b) to
c) with
d) without

19 The doctor suggested ___ .

a) me to stop smoking
b) that I stop smoking
c) that I stop to smoke
d) me to stop to smoke

20 "Are you sure you don't want to go?"
" ... like to, I have another appointment."

a) As much as I
b) Much as I'd
c) Much as I
d) More than I'd

Part II Key word transformation

Follow the same instructions as in Exam Practice 1

1 If it had not been for your assistance, I wouldn't have made it to the top. **(were)**

__________________________ for your assistance, I wouldn't have made it to the top.

2 There is very little evidence to support his accusations. **(hardly)**

There is __________________________ his accusations.

3 She was an excellent teacher, but the students didn't like her. **(despite)**

__________________________ teacher, the students didn't like her.

4 I wasn't able attend the meeting because I was taken ill to hospital. **(make)**

I __________________________ meeting because I was taken ill to hospital.

5 I didn't hand in my homework because I had forgotten to do it. **(having)**

__________________________, I didn't hand it in.

6 I'd prefer to stay at home rather than go out on a rainy day. **(sooner)**

__________________________ out on a rainy day.

7 If the president resigned, I would take over as Head of Department. **(were)**

__________________________, I would take over as Head of Department.

8 John isn't nearly as hard working as his brother. **(much)**
John's brother ____________________________.

9 In addition to singing well, she is a gifted poet. **(but)**
Not only ____________________________ a gifted poet.

10 I expected more students to attend the lecture. **(fewer)**
There ____________________________ I expected.

ROUND OFF 2

1 Match the columns to find the antonyms:

a) boastful	**f)** aloof
b) disreputable	**g)** thrive
c) lukewarm	**h)** notorious
d) mischievous	**i)** inconsequential
e) parsimonious	**j)** parochial

1) ___ gregarious, sociable
2) ___ decline, decrease
3) ___ liberal, broad
4) ___ honorable, respected, decent
5) ___ generous, lavish
6) ___ enthusiastic, excited
7) ___ significant, important
8) ___ humble, modest, reserved
9) ___ unimportant, unknown
10) ___ well behaved, obedient

2 Match the words from A – J above with one of these synonyms:

1) ___ infamous
2) ___ unfriendly
3) ___ bragging
4) ___ flourish
5) ___ playful
6) ___ discreditable
7) ___ unimportant
8) ___ apathetic
9) ___ opinionated
10) ___ stingy

3 Choose the correct collocation pattern:

1) to have a(n) ___ eye
A) pervasive B) biased C) cursory D) unerring

2) ___ looks
A) unflattering B) engrossed C) hazardous D) impassable

3) a(n) ___ inspection
A) biased B) cursory C) saturated D) baffling

4) ___ an offensive smell
A) wear off B) gauge C) give off D) put off

5) to be ___ in a book
A) engrossed B) unruly C) assertive D) pervasive

6) ___ murders
A) risqué B) affordable C) grisly D) cursory

7) dance with ___
A) penchant B) panache C) pursuit D) dwelling

8) ___ with rage
A) seethe B) pursuit C) gauge D) neglect

9) a(n) ___ question
A) pussyfoot B) unflattering C) baffling D) unerring

10) ___ your memory
A) ensure B) boost C) pester D) depict

4 Match the answers from 3 with one of these synonyms or definitions:

a) ___ emit
b) ___ uninteresting
c) ___ gruesome, ghastly
d) ___ slapdash, careless
e) ___ flair, skillfulness
f) ___ unfailing (to realize something)
g) ___ increase
h) ___ absorbed, immersed
i) ___ bewildering, perplexing
j) ___ boil, simmer

5 WORD FORMATION – Complete the table with the forms which are missing. If one of the forms doesn't exist, fill in the space with an X:

NOUN	VERB	ADJECTIVE	ADVERB
		boastful	
		mischievous	
		parsimonious	
	thrive		
			thoroughly
		pervasive	
		aloof	
	neglect		
		hazardous	
	afford		

Key to lessons 6 – 10

LESSON 6 – a) 10 b) 3 c) 6 d) 8 e) 1 f) 2 g) 4 h) 5 i) 9 j) 7
LESSON 7 – a) 9 b) 3 c) 1 d) 7 e) 10 f) 5 g) 6 h) 2 i) 4 j) 8
LESSON 8 – a) 1 b) 5 c) 8 d) 4 e) 10 f) 7 g) 2 h) 3 i) 9 j) 6
LESSON 9 – a) 2 b) 7 c) 8 d) 6 e) 1 f) 3 g) 5 h) 4 i) 9 j) 1
LESSON 10 – a) 6 b) 4 c) 5 d) 1 e) 7 f) 10 g) 2 h) 3 i) 8 j) 9

EXAM PRACTICE 2

PART I

1 B) "But" in this case is close in meaning to "except".

2 D) (= "The teacher was not sure if she would punish him.") After "as to", only "whether" (and not "if") is possible.

3 C) If the first clause contains "would have" + participle, the next clause is generally used in the past perfect, if the situation is already over.

4 B) For emphasis, after the phrase "not only", we use the interrogative structure (inversion of word order)

5 A) "Which" replaces the subject of the previous sentence. "That" cannot come in a "non-defining clause".

6 D) We do not normally use "will" in the "if clause". It is used here to emphasize willingness or to show politeness.

7 A) We insert "adverbs" or "adverb phrases" after the first "auxiliary verb": "you have *always/never/seldom etc...* been".

8 D) "Whose" is the only option that indicates possession.

9 B) We use the present perfect to talk about things which started in the past and continue into the present.

10 B) (= "After everything else has been considered, it is the people who are...")

11 D) We use "for" (and not "since"), when we want to emphasize duration.

12 A) (= "A microscope enables scientists to observe...") If we use the verb "make" to express similar meaning, it is followed by a preparatory object "it" + "for" + subject.

13 D) (= "The objective of this study is to throw light...") The possible structures are: "aim [VERB] to do" or "be aimed at doing".

14 B) After the frequency adverb "rarely", we use the interrogative structure (inversion of word order) for emphasis.

15 B) (= "Those <u>who are</u> signing up for the exam...") We can cross out the adjective clause (underlined) and use the gerund as an adjective.

16 D) We use the preposition "in" for the seasons of the year.

17 C) (= "It wasn't possible for me to go to the party because...")
18 B) "To make it up to someone" means "to compensate".
19 B) (= "... that I <u>should</u> stop smoking.") "Suggest" cannot be followed by an object pronoun (me, you, him etc.).) "Should" is rarely used in this sense in American English.
20 B) (= "I would like to, <u>but</u> ...")

PART II

1 ***Were it not***
2 ***hardly any evidence to support.***
3 ***Despite the fact that she was an excellent***
4 ***couldn't make it to the***
5 ***Having forgotten to do my homework***
6 ***I'd sooner stay at home than go***
7 ***Were the president to resign***
8 ***is much more hard working than him*** (or ***than he is***)
9 ***does she sing well, but she is also***
10 ***were fewer students attending the lecture than***

ROUNDING OFF 2

1 1 f 2 g 3 j 4 b 5 e 6 c 7 i 8 a 9 h 10) d
2 1) b 2) f 3) a 4) g 5) d 6) h 7) i 8) c 9) j 10) e
3 1) d 2) a 3) b 4) c 5) a 6) c 7) b 8) a 9) c 10) b
4 a) 4 b) 2 c) 6 d) 3 e) 7 f) 1 g) 10 h) 5 i) 9 j) 8
5 WORD FORMATION

NOUN	VERB	ADJECTIVE	ADVERB
boastfulness	boast	***boastful***	boastfully
mischievousness	x	***mischievous***	mischievously
parsimony	x	***parsimonious***	parsimoniously
x	***thrive***	thriving	x
thoroughness		thorough	***thoroughly***
pervasiveness	pervade	***pervasive***	pervasively
aloofness	x	***aloof***	x
negligence	***neglect***	negligent, neglectful	negligently
hazard	x	***hazardous***	x
x	***afford***	affordable	x

10 MINUTES A DAY

LESSON 11

Stage 1 Read the sentences carefully and try to figure out the meaning of the word or expression in bold from the context. Then, go on to the next Stage.

1 In Brazil, there's a ***pernicious*** interference of politicians who want to bring censorship back.
2 Paris, the capital of France, is the ***epitome*** of a sophisticated city.
3 We cannot be ***complacent*** about our academic performance. We still have a long way to go.
4 It is ***disheartening*** for classic music singers to see what young people enjoy nowadays.
5 The party's political campaign was full of lies and ***deceit***.
6 We will ***endeavor*** to do our very best to help you in any way we can.
7 Many workers were made ***redundant*** when the company went bankrupt.
8 The witnesses ***corroborated*** the evidence presented by the prosecutors.
9 I used to have a wide circle of ***acquaintances*** when I was at university.
10 The teacher's ***overbearing*** personality made her students feel insecure and downtrodden.

Stage 2 Match the words and expressions with their definitions or synonyms:

a) ___ [VERB]: make efforts, strive
b) ___ [NOUN]: the best example of
c) ___ [ADJECTIVE]: domineering, authoritarian, dictatorial
d) ___ [VERB]: confirm
e) ___ [ADJECTIVE]: sad, disappointing, depressing
f) ___ [ADJECTIVE]: unnecessary, unemployed
g) ___ [ADJECTIVE]: smug, self-satisfied
h) ___ [NOUN]: deception, the act of making someone believe what is not true
i) ___ [ADJECTIVE]: very harmful
j) ___ [NOUN]: friends you only know slightly

10 MINUTES A DAY

LESSON 12

Stage 1 Read the sentences carefully and try to figure out the meaning of the word or expression in bold from the context. Then, go on to the next Stage.

1 Everyone liked the worker in the company. He was very ***obliging*** and good-hearted.
2 With ***hindsight***, I don't regret what I've done, although I wish things had been different.
3 I had a hunch of ***impending*** disaster on the day which the ship departed.
4 Those ***obnoxious***, stupid students made the teacher leave her job.
5 A ***cauldron*** of corruption in politics was about to become a sensation in newspapers scandals.
6 John was a ***hack*** who wouldn't spare anyone in his malicious reports.
7 Depressed, Lisa contemplated her ***bleak*** future in the company.
8 The ***abrasiveness*** of his reviews in the newspaper disturbed the writers.
9 His ***anodyne*** writing needed a lot of practice to become more attractive to readers.
10 Peter was a ***seasoned*** lawyer whose prestige was known everywhere.

Stage 2 Match the words and expressions with their definitions or synonyms:

a) ___ **[NOUN]**: pot (figuratively: an unstable, dangerous situation)
b) ___ **[NOUN]**: unkindness, rudeness, harshness
c) ___ **[ADJECTIVE]**: loathsome, unpleasant character, detestable
d) ___ **[ADJECTIVE]**: experienced, skillful
e) ___ **[NOUN]**: an unscrupulous journalist who only writes for the money
f) ___ **[ADJECTIVE]**: extremely willing to be helpful, accommodating
g) ___ **[ADJECTIVE]**: looming, upcoming, imminent
h) ___ **[NOUN]**: in retrospective
i) ___ **[ADJECTIVE]**: gloomy, dismal, unpromising
j) ___ **[ADJECTIVE]**: bland, unexciting

10 MINUTES A DAY

LESSON 13

Stage 1 Read the sentences carefully and try to figure out the meaning of the word or expression in bold from the context. Then, go on to the next Stage.

1 The witness's ***poignant*** testimony left the jury on the verge of tears.
2 Everyone sneered at the ***preposterousness*** of the plan.
3 Kittens play all the time to ***hone*** their instinctive skills.
4 I ***abhor*** prejudice of any kind. I just can't tolerate it.
5 The controversial artist is known for his ***acerbity*** in his declarations to the press.
6 The teacher couldn't put up with the children's ***naughty*** behavior.
7 I've asked the teacher to ***rectify*** my grades. They're all wrong.
8 Although I am not ***averse*** to vegetarian diets, I still prefer meat.
9 The young man's ***disheveled*** appearance cost him a job opportunity.
10 A truly confident friend would never ***divulge*** what he's told.

Stage 2 Match the words and expressions with their definitions or synonyms:

a) ___ **[NOUN]**: foolishness, silliness
b) ___ **[ADJECTIVE]**: heartbreaking, moving
c) ___ **[ADJECTIVE]**: reluctant, disinclined
d) ___ **[VERB]**: set right, correct
e) ___ **[VERB]**: loathe, despise, detest, strongly dislike
f) ___ **[VERB]**: tell, reveal (a secret)
g) ___ **[VERB]**: sharpen (figuratively: enhance, improve, perfect)
h) ___ **[NOUN]**: sourness (figuratively: bitter, critical humor)
i) ___ **[ADJECTIVE]**: untidy
j) ___ **[ADJECTIVE]**: bad

10 MINUTES A DAY

LESSON 14

Stage 1 Read the sentences carefully and try to figure out the meaning of the word or expression in bold from the context. Then, go on to the next Stage.

1 He was a tough, ***uncompromising*** man who would never change his mind.
2 The student regarded himself as an ***outcast***, so he distanced himself from the rest of the class.
3 I was trying to ***pluck up*** courage to jump from the bridge into the water.
4 The caring mother was responsible for the children's ***upbringing***.
5 After ***painstaking*** analysis of the evidence, the detective reached a conclusion.
6 The ***fierce*** competition in today's society is leading us into depression.
7 He was ***presumably*** the one responsible for the attacks.
8 The scientific project has ***come up against*** a lot of criticism.
9 The chief executive was expelled accused of ***swindle***.
10 At the end of the 19 century, Paris lived an era of ***affluence*** and glamour.

Stage 2 Match the words and expressions with their definitions or synonyms:

a) ___ [NOUN]: opulence, abundance, prosperity
b) ___ [ADJECTIVE]: cutthroat, ruthless, ferocious
c) ___ [NOUN]: deception, fraud
d) ___ [ADJECTIVE]: stubborn, intransigent, inflexible
e) ___ [ADJECTIVE]: thorough, precise, complete
f) ___ [ADVERB]: supposedly true
g) ___ [NOUN]: training, teaching
h) ___ [VERB]: gather, summon, muster
i) ___ [VERB]: meet with, be opposed
j) ___ [NOUN]: unaccepted by the social group

10 MINUTES A DAY

LESSON 15

Stage 1 Read the sentences carefully and try to figure out the meaning of the word or expression in bold from the context. Then, go on to the next Stage.

1 They paid ***homage*** to John Lennon by inviting several artists to sing his songs.
2 The ***ineluctable*** nature of death makes us humans feel so fragile.
3 The theatrical company's ***rendition*** of that Shakespearean classic was a consummate success.
4 The criminal ***absconded*** with the money and remained at large for a long time.
5 That mysterious gypsy's predictions had a ***baleful*** influence on the famous actress's life.
6 You won't be able to keep your ***complicity*** in this plot a secret for much longer.
7 The worker's ***deferential*** manners towards everyone made him a popular friend in the company.
8 John's ***dauntless*** enthusiasm for the project was so contagious and unwavering.
9 The politician ***egregious*** mistake was a hazard to his candidature.
10 When interrogated by the police, the woman would only give ***elusive*** answers.

Stage 2 Match the words and expressions with their definitions or synonyms:

a) ___ [NOUN]: involvement
b) ___ [ADJECTIVE]: noticeable, extremely bad
c) ___ [NOUN]: performance
d) ___ [ADJECTIVE]: evasive, hard to understand
e) ___ [ADJECTIVE]: respectful, polite
f) ___ [NOUN]: tribute, honor
g) ___ [ADJECTIVE]: irresistible (that cannot be resisted, opposed), inescapable
h) ___ [VERB]: run away, escape
i) ___ [ADJECTIVE]: ominous, threateningly evil
j) ___ [ADJECTIVE]: bold, courageous, intrepid

EXAM PRACTICE 3
GRAMMAR

Part 1 Multiple-choice

1 If I ___ an opportunity, I wouldn't have missed it.

a) would have
b) will have
c) had
d) had had

2 I've told you ___ to stay away from that obnoxious man.

a) many a time
b) many's time
c) many a times
d) much times

3 Would you be so kind ___ help me?

a) as to
b) so to
c) as for
d) so that

4 Don't eat with your mouth open, ___?

a) shall you
b) will you
c) won't you
d) do you

5 The doctor told me ___ smoke.

a) to not
b) don't
c) not to
d) not

6 What I did was ___ him to leave.

a) telling
b) that I told
c) to tell
d) told

7 Why don't you try to look ___ the bright side of things?

a) at
b) to
c) for
d) on

8 You can use either an infinitive ___ a gerund after this verb.

a) and
b) or
c) nor
d) but

9 I had already been introduced to some of the students ___the lecture.
a) whom attended
b) which attended
c) attending
d) to attend

10 I hope I can count ___ your understanding.
a) on
b) with
c) for
d) in

11 ___ the opportunity, I would've traveled more.
a) Had I
b) I had
c) Had I had
d) Have I had

12 You are supposed to fill in the form ___ ink.
a) with
b) in
c) on
d) by

13 The movie ___ was inspired by a true story.
a) I told you about it
b) about I told you
c) that I told you about
d) which I told you about it

14 ___ for her intelligence, we wouldn't have solved the problem.
a) Had it not been
b) Although
c) Wouldn't it
d) Unless it was

15 ___ told me what was happening, I could have helped you.

a) Should you have

b) Would you had

c) At least you had

d) If only you had

16 "I am so worried!"

"___."

a) So do I.

b) So am I.

c) I do, too.

d) Me neither.

17 The student worked really hard ___ a scholarship to study abroad.

a) so as to get

b) for to get

c) to getting

d) in order to getting

18 What ___ to your hair? You look awful!

a) did you do

b) have you done

c) had you done

d) do you do

19 ___ of these books do you prefer?

a) What

b) Which

c) Which ones

d) What ones

20 The burglar ___ by the police.

a) is rumored to have been killed

b) is rumored to have killed

c) is rumored to had been killed

d) is rumored has been killed

Part 2 Key word transformation

Follow the same instructions as in Exam Practice 1.

1 They have not rescued any of the survivors so far. **(yet)**
None of the survivors ___________________________.

2 The student is working hard to get a high pass. **(as)**
The student is working hard ___________________________ a low pass.

3 He is the most petulant person I've ever met! **(anyone)**
I've ___________________________ him.

4 I don't like her, but I must admit that she's competent. **(spite)**
In ___________________________ like her, I must admit that she's competent.

5 I wish you would learn to prepare your own meals. **(high)**
It's ___________________________ your own meals.

6 If only you had enjoyed life more when you were younger. **(taken)**
I wish ___________________________ life more when you were younger.

7 I think it would be better if you solved the problem yourself. **(prefer)**
I'd ___________________________ the problem yourself.

8 If you don't rub out wrong answers carefully, your grade will be penalized. **(otherwise)**
Rub out ___________________________ your grade will be penalized.

9 They didn't realize something was going wrong until the lights went out. **(did)**
Only ___________________________ something was going wrong.

10 You shouldn't forget to hand in your homework tomorrow. **(account)**
On ___________________________ to hand in your homework tomorrow.

ROUND OFF 3

1 Try to remember the meaning of the words below. To help you, we've given you some typical collocation patterns in which these words can usually be found:

1) pernicious
2) corroborated
3) bleak
4) anodyne
5) poignant
6) preposterousness
7) painstaking
8) affluence
9) ineluctable
10) elusive

a) ___ ~ tendency
b) ___ ~ the facts
c) ___ ~ influence
d) ___ ~ testimony

e) ___ an era of ~
f) ___ ~ climate, future
g) ___ ~ of an idea
h) ___ ~ criticism
i) ___ ~ study, analysis
j) ___ ~ answers, explanations

2 Now match question one numbers (1 – 10) with the meanings or definitions:

a) ___ inescapable
b) ___ wealth
c) ___ damaging, harmful
d) ___ confirm
e) ___ gloomy, depressive
f) ___ moving, which causes strong emotions
g) ___ bland, unexciting
h) ___ carefully detailed, thorough, precise
i) ___ ludicrousness, stupidity
j) ___ evasive, difficult to grasp

3 Fill in the spaces with one of the following words:

complacent	***uncompromising***
overbearing	***rendition***
hindsight	***baleful***
obnoxious	***deferential***
hone	***dauntless***

a) The world is now experiencing the ___ effects of the ozone layer destruction.
b) With ___, I can now understand my decision was right.
c) Whenever anyone criticized his slapdash work, he'd only give a ___ smile.
d) It's useless to try to negotiate with our teacher. She's ___ when it comes to schoolwork deadlines.

e) The ___ leader guided the demonstrations against the government's policies.

f) The principal administered the school so well because he was feared for his ___ personality.

g) Japanese students were once thought to be excessively ___ to teachers.

h) The weird student would spend a long time by himself ___ his skills in chess.

i) This has to be the best ___ of a Shakespearean play I've ever seen.

j) Our father was a somewhat ___ man who was never satisfied with anything.

4 Match the words from the sentences below (1 – 8) with a definition or synonym (A – H):

1) It was disheartening for the student to see his poor grades.

2) Many workers were made redundant due to the economic crisis.

3) I used to have a wide circle of friends and acquaintances at the university.

4) The seasoned teacher was used to working with students from all walks of life.

5) Even though I'm not averse to different cultures, I don't like trying new kinds of food.

6) His passionate character was strongly influenced by his upbringing in a Latin American country.

7) The robbers absconded with the money stolen from the bank.

8) The teacher who marked my composition said I had made some egregious grammar mistakes.

a) ___ to have a strong dislike/opposition to something

b) ___ no longer employed because work is unavailable

c) ___ instruction provided by parents to their children

d) ___ something that makes you lose determination

e) ___ something that is outstanding in a bad way

f) ___ accustomed to particular conditions, experienced

g) ___ a person who you know only slightly and is not a close friend

h) ___ to hide in order to avoid being captured or prosecuted

5 WORD FORMATION

NOUN	VERB	ADJECTIVE	ADVERB
	corroborate		
		poignant	
affluence			
		elusive	
abhor			
averse			
			presumably
complicity			
		deferential	
acerbity			

Key to lessons 11 – 15

LESSON 11 – a) 6 b) 2 c) 10 d) 8 e) 4 f) 7 g) 3 h) 5 i) 1 j) 9
LESSON 12 – a) 5 b) 8 c) 4 d) 10 e) 6 f) 1 g) 3 h) 2 i) 7 j) 9
LESSON 13 – a) 2 b) 1 c) 8 d) 7 e) 4 f) 10 g) 3 h) 5 i) 9 j) 6
LESSON 14 – a) 10 b) 6 c) 9 d) 1 e) 5 f) 7 g) 4 h) 3 i) 8 j) 2
LESSON 15 – a) 6 b) 9 c) 3 d) 10 e) 7 f) 1 g) 2 h) 4 i) 5 j) 8

EXAM PRACTICE 3

PART I

1 D) If the main clause is formed with "would (not) have + participle", the past perfect is used in the "if- clause".
2 A) (= many times) (Formal)
3 A) The phrase "Would you be so kind" (formal) is always followed by "as to".
4 B) In negative imperatives, "will you" is used in the tag question.
5 C) The direct speech would read as: "... don't smoke." In indirect speech, "don't" becomes "not to".
6 C) The phrase "What I did" works as the subject of the sentence. Sentences like these are followed either by the "to infinitive" or the "bare infinitive": "What I did was (to) tell him to leave."
7 D) Collocation pattern
8 B) This is a parallel structure: "either ... or".
9 C) (= "... to some of the students who were attending the lecture."). It is possible to cross out the adjective clause (underlined) and use the gerund as an adjective.
10 A) In this sense, the verb "count" always takes the preposition "on".
11 C) (= "If I had had the opportunity...") "If" was dropped out and the interrogative structure was used.
12 B) Always use this preposition in this expression.
13 C) (= "I told you about the movie. It was inspired by a true story".) "A" would be correct without "it" at the end; "B" is not a natural construction; "D", like "A", would be correct if we dropped "it".
14 A) (= "If it had not been for her..."). For emphasis, "if" was omitted and then the interrogative structure was used.
15 D) (= "I wish you had told me..."). We use "if only" to add emphasis.
16 B) (= "I am, too.")
17 A) It would also be possible: "The student worked really hard to get / in order to get a scholarship..."

18 B) We use the present perfect to show how something in the past affects the present (she looks awful <u>now</u> because she had her haircut).
19 B) We use "which" when we ask about a limited number of options.
20 A) (= "It is rumored that the burglar has been killed by the police.")

PART II

1 ***have been rescued as yet***
2 ***so as not to get***
3 ***never met anyone as petulant as***
4 ***spite of the fact that I don't***
5 ***high time you learned to prepare***
6 ***you had taken the chance to enjoy***
7 ***it if you solved***
8 ***wrong answers carefully, otherwise***
9 ***when the lights went out did they realize***
10 ***no account should you forget***

ROUNDING OFF 3

1 a) 9 b) 2 c) 1 d) 5 e) 8 f) 3 g) 6 h) 4 i) 7 j) 10
2 a) 9 b) 8 c) 1 d) 2 e) 3 f) 5 g) 4 h) 7 i) 6 j) 10
3 a) baleful b) hindsight c) complacent d) uncompromising e) dauntless f) overbearing g) deferential h) honing i) rendition j) obnoxious
4 a) 5 b) 2 c) 6 d) a e) 8 f) 4 g) 3 h) 7
5 WORD FORMATION

NOUN	VERB	ADJECTIVE	ADVERB
corroboration	***corroborate***	corroborative	x
poignancy	x	***poignant***	poignantly
affluence	x	affluent	x
elusiveness	elude	***elusive***	elusively
abhorrence	***abhor***	abhorrent	x
aversion	x	***averse***	x
presumption	presume	presumable	***presumably***
complicity	x	accomplice	x
deference	x	***deferential***	deferentially
acerbity	x	acerbic	x

10 MINUTES A DAY

LESSON 16

Stage 1 Read the sentences carefully and try to figure out the meaning of the word or expression in bold from the context. Then, go on to the next Stage.

1 The soccer players arrived at their destination prior to the match so they could ***acclimatize*** themselves to the place.
2 The students ***exulted*** at being awarded honor certificates.
3 This adventurous journey is ***fraught*** with dangers of all sorts.
4 The players regarded their defeat as ***ignominious*** and unjustifiable.
5 We need your ***judicious*** advice to help us make the right decision.
6 I didn't like the play because of the cast's ***lackluster*** performance.
7 It is ***mandatory*** for students to hand in an end term paper at the end of the semester.
8 After the tornadoes, people were worried about the attacks of ***marauders*** trying to loot everything they could.
9 The lawyer was clearly trying to ***obfuscate*** the evidence given by the witnesses.
10 The witnesses were warned by the judge that they might serve a sentence for ***perjury***.

Stage 2 Match the words and expressions with their definitions or synonyms:

a) ___ [VERB]: deliberately make something hard to understand
b) ___ [ADJECTIVE]: wise, good judgment
c) ___ [NOUN]: a lie under solemn oath in a court of law
d) ___ [ADJECTIVE]: compulsory, obligatory
e) ___ [ADJECTIVE]: shameful, humiliating
f) ___ [VERB]: get used to, adapt
g) ___ [VERB]: show great happiness
h) ___ [ADJECTIVE]: dull, uninspired
i) ___ [ADJECTIVE]: filled with
j) ___ [NOUN]: a group of dangerous raiders

10 MINUTES A DAY

LESSON 17

Stage 1 Read the sentences carefully and try to figure out the meaning of the word or expression in bold from the context. Then, go on to the next Stage.

1 I'm not going to ***demean*** myself by begging you to forgive me.
2 No one knew what conclusion to arrive at after the ***contentious*** debate.
3 I am now ***worse off*** financially than when I was a student.
4 These ***industrious*** workers are the company's pride, they're always willing to do their best.
5 The media now witnesses a ***backlash*** against predatory marketing.
6 The company is ***thriving*** after a long period of recession. Workers aren't worried about losing their jobs any longer.
7 In its ***heyday***, this company used to offer jobs to more than 1000 workers.
8 Children's behavior in school nowadays is so ***appalling***.
9 You shouldn't indulge in ***complacency***. Your work still needs improvement.
10 Students who come from a poor background are ***eligible*** for a university scholarship.

Stage 2 Match the words and expressions with their definitions or synonyms:

a) ___ [VERB]: belittle, humiliate
b) ___ [ADJECTIVE]: shocking, disgusting
c) ___ [NOUN]: successful time, period
d) ___ [ADJECTIVE]: entitled, qualified
e) ___ [ADJECTIVE]: less wealthy
f) ___ [VERB]: prosper, develop successfully
g) ___ [NOUN]: negative reaction, revolt
h) ___ [ADJECTIVE]: hard-working
i) ___ [ADJECTIVE]: arguable, disputable, debatable
j) ___ [NOUN]: undeserved self-satisfaction

10 MINUTES A DAY

LESSON 18

Stage 1 Read the sentences carefully and try to figure out the meaning of the word or expression in bold from the context. Then, go on to the next Stage.

1 The candidate's composed ***demeanor*** made him a favorite among the electorate.
2 In order to win a ***scholarship***, you need to have good grades.
3 The family's ***thrifty*** spending habits is what help them go through hardship.
4 The students remained ***apathetic***, no matter what the teacher did.
5 The teacher worked hard to ***live up to*** his students' expectations, but it was no good.
6 ***Whereas*** some people received the book with enthusiasm, others have found it quite boring.
7 We're making efforts to ***foster*** a feeling of commitment among the team players.
8 The unscrupulous scientists had an ***insatiable*** desire for fame and fortune.
9 He put it to her in ***blunt*** language he didn't like her.
10 The university is ***comprised*** of four main faculties.

Stage 2 Match the words and expressions with their definitions or synonyms:

a) ___ [VERB]: fulfill, be what something/someone is expected to be
b) ___ [ADJECTIVE]: voracious, which cannot be satisfied
c) ___ [NOUN]: money given by a school to help students pay for expenses
d) ___ [ADJECTIVE]: straightforward, direct
e) ___ [ADJECTIVE]: sparing, economical
f) ___ [VERB]: promote, develop
g) ___ [NOUN]: behavior
h) ___ [ADJECTIVE]: impassive, unenthusiastic
i) ___ [ADJECTIVE]: made up of, consist of
j) ___ [CONJUNCTION]: while (to express a comparison)

10 MINUTES A DAY

LESSON 19

Stage 1 Read the sentences carefully and try to figure out the meaning of the word or expression in bold from the context. Then, go on to the next Stage.

1 His ***tactful*** choice of words not to hurt people's feeling is admirable.
2 After painstaking analysis, we've found out some ***discrepancy*** in the information given.
3 Because he's a ***teetotaler***, his health is incredible even at his advanced age.
4 I don't want to bear the ***burden*** of being responsible for the failure of the project.
5 The soil is now ***impoverished*** after many years of poor farming practices.
6 She was ***plagued*** by a feeling of guilt throughout her life.
7 The hills are only ***sparsely*** covered with thin vegetation.
8 He's a very ***conscientious*** teacher. He makes a point of returning the exams as soon as possible.
9 A ***bewildering*** amount of information had to be analyzed carefully before we could proceed with the process.
10 The criminal was pleaded innocent for ***dearth*** of evidence.

Stage 2 Match the words and expressions with their definitions or synonyms:

a) ___ [ADJECTIVE]: perplexing
b) ___ [VERB]: pestered, annoyed, tormented
c) ___ [NOUN]: scarcity, paucity, lack
d) ___ [NOUN]: a person who never drinks alcohol.
e) ___ [NOUN]: inconsistency
f) ___ [NOUN]: pressure, strain
g) ___ [ADJECTIVE]: careful not to offend people
h) ___ [ADJECTIVE]: aware of one's responsibilities at work
i) ___ [ADVERB]: small in number, spread out over an area
j) ___ [ADJECTIVE]: made poor

10 MINUTES A DAY

LESSON 20

Stage 1 Read the sentences carefully and try to figure out the meaning of the word or expression in bold from the context. Then, go on to the next Stage.

1 The bride's family threw a ***lavish*** party which suitably impressed the guests.
2 We had to be careful about every ***minute*** detail in the research process.
3 The youth ***yearns*** for even more freedom from the dictatorship of models.
4 "Your performance in the audition was just ***passable***," said the director.
5 The city was full of ***derelict*** buildings in a run-down area.
6 Alcohol consumption often leads to ***disruptive*** behavior.
7 A ***scholarly*** man, Peter was admired by everyone at the university.
8 ***Virtually*** everyone has a mobile phone nowadays.
9 The public is waiting anxiously for the writer's ***forthcoming*** book.
10 I had to ***withdraw*** what I had said to avoid further problems with my boss.

Stage 2 Match the words and expressions with their definitions or synonyms:

a) ___ [VERB]: take back, retract
b) ___ [ADJECTIVE]: uncared for, in bad condition
c) ___ [VERB]: long, wait eagerly for something
d) ___ [ADJECTIVE]: grand, elaborate, impressive
e) ___ [ADJECTIVE]: learned, intellectual
f) ___ [ADJECTIVE]: tiny, small
g) ___ [ADVERB]: practically, almost
h) ___ [ADJECTIVE]: adequate, fair
i) ___ [ADJECTIVE]: abnormal
j) ___ [ADJECTIVE]: appearing soon

EXAM PRACTICE 4
GRAMMAR

Part 1 Multiple-choice

1 I can lend you my book ___ you help me with homework.

a) as long
b) so long as
c) just in case
d) unless

2 I ___ up late because I had a lot of homework to do.

a) was made stay
b) made to stay
c) was made staying
d) was made to stay

3 I ___ to school on foot every day.
a) used to going
b) am used to go
c) go usually
d) would go

4 I'm having my house ___ these days.
a) renovated
b) renovate
c) renovates
d) to renovate

5 ___ a rainy day, we stayed home lazing around.
a) For being
b) It being
c) To be
d) Since was

6 Do you think there's any chance of ___ an accident?
a) there being
b) there to be
c) there is
d) there are

7 He stopped ___ alcohol on his doctor's advice.
a) to drink
b) drinking
c) drink
d) the drink

8 There ___ seem to be any evidence to support his theory.
a) isn't
b) aren't
c) don't
d) doesn't

9 I suggested ___ an optician immediately.
a) him see
b) he to see
c) that he see
d) him saw

10 I won't speak to you again ___.
a) unless you apologize
b) if you apologize
c) even though you apologize
d) would you apologize

11 There's ___ any possibility of the students passing the exam.
a) virtually
b) clearly
c) hardly
d) practically

12 I would appreciate ___ more polite towards everyone.
a) it if you were
b) if you were
c) that you were
d) you if you were

13 ___ hard she tried, she didn't succeed in changing the tire.
a) Although
b) Whatever
c) However
d) Whenever

14 Interesting ___ your idea is, I don't think it will work.
a) than
b) but
c) how
d) as

15 I've heard ___ that he has been arrested.

a) saying
b) it said
c) said
d) to say

16 Within ten years' time I ___ .

a) am retiring
b) retire
c) will have been retired
d) will have retired

17 How ___ is allowed on the flight?

a) much baggage
b) many baggages
c) many luggages
d) much luggages

18 "Why have you chosen Paul to be the leader?"
"Because ___ not only sings but performs very well."

a) he does
b) does he
c) is he
d) he

19 "Ann looks exhausted. What do you think happened?"
"She must ___ late last night working on the reports."

a) stay up
b) have stayed up
c) had stayed up
d) has stayed up

20 The headlines say the mayor ___.

a) is resign

b) is to resign
c) is to be resigned
d) is resigned

Part 2 Key word transformation

Follow the same instructions as in Exam Practice 1.

1 I had only just arrived when he movie started. **(sooner)**
No ____________________________ the movie started.

2 Encouraging physical exercise is something that must be done urgently. **(what)**
Encouraging physical exercise is ____________________________.

3 Proctors may disqualify any candidate who gets caught cheating. **(whoever)**
Proctors are ____________________________ gets caught cheating.

4 I haven't seen you for such a long time! **(ago)**
The last time I ____________________________.

5 I've never been here before. **(time)**
This is the ____________________________ here.

6 He was the most intelligent student in the class. **(anyone)**
There ____________________________ him in the class.

7 I'm dying to go to Brazil. **(forward)**
I ____________________________ to Brazil.

8 I asked my sister to answer the door for me because I was busy. **(had)**
I ____________________________ for me because I was busy.

9 I think you should leave for work now. **(time)**
It's __________________________ for work.

10 Scientists will certainly find a cure for cancer. **(bound)**
Scientists __________________________ a cure for cancer.

ROUND OFF 4

1 Browse through units 16 – 20 to search for the word which correctly fits in the gaps below.

There is a synonym or definition at the end of each sentence to help you.

a) I find it hard to ___ myself to the mountain climate. (***get used to***)

b) I hope I can count on your __________ advice to help us. (***wise***)

c) Your _______ writing can be improved by intensive practice. (***unexciting***)

d) Everyone praised him at the company for his __________ work. (***hard--working***)

e) Adolescents are prone to _________ behavior if they start taking drugs. (***abnormal***)

f) They received the tragic news with a composed __________. (***posture, manner***)

g) Students who come from poorer countries are _______ for a scholarship to help them pay for
their expenses. (***qualified, entitled***)

h) I'm a __________ consumer. I only buy what's essential. (***spending money carefully***)

i) Due to the ________ of food, the animals are starving to death. (***scarcity***)

j) __________ workers try to do their duties carefully. (***careful to work properly***)

2 Match the two halves:

a) fraught	1) with danger
b) mandatory	2) of proof
c) demean	3) shows
d) backlash	4) theories
e) appalling	5) learning
f) foster	6) what you say
g) burden	7) rules
h) bewildering	8) conduct
i) withdraw	9) yourself
j) forthcoming	10) against corruption

3 Match the words from A – J from exercise 2 with one of these synonyms or definitions:

1) ___ create
2) ___ filled
3) ___ load
4) ___ compulsory
5) ___ shocking
6) ___ perplexing
7) ___ arranged to happen soon
8) ___ belittle
9) ___ revolt
10) ___ retract

4 WORD FORMATION

NOUN	VERB	ADJECTIVE	ADVERB
		judicious	
	obfuscate		
	demean		
		thriving	
		complacent	
		eligible	
		tactful	
discrepancy			
		bewildering	
		disruptive	

Key to lessons 16 – 20

LESSON 16 – a) 9 b) 5 c) 10 d) 7 e) 4 f) 1 g) 2 h) 6 i) 3 j) 8
LESSON 17 – a) 1 b) 8 c) 7 d) 10 e) 3 f) 6 g) 5 h) 4 i) 2 j) 9
LESSON 18 – a) 5 b) 8 c) 2 d) 9 e) 3 f) 7 g) 1 h) 4 i) 10 j) 6
LESSON 19 – a) 9 b) 6 c) 10 d) 3 e) 2 f) 4 g) 1 h) 8 i) 7 j) 5
LESSON 20 – a) 10 b) 5 c) 3 d) 1 e) 7 f) 2 g) 8 h) 4 i) 6 j) 9

EXAM PRACTICE 4

PART I

1 B) (= "as long as")
2 D) In the passive, the verb "make" is always followed by the infinitive with "to".
3 D) We use "would" to show that something was a habit in the past.
4 A) (= "My house is being renovated by...") This is called the causative use of "have".
5 B) (= "Because it was a rainy day...")
6 A) The gerund is used after the preparatory subject "there" because of the preposition "of".
7 B) After "stop", we use the gerund to say that something has ceased to happen.
8 D) (= "It seems that there isn't any evidence...")
9 C) The verb "see" is used in the bare infinitive because it is in the subjunctive. In British English, we can see "should" implicit before "see": "I suggested that he <u>should</u> see an optician..."
10 A) (= "if you don't apologize") "Unless" means the same as "if not".
11 C) That is, the chances are too slim.
12 A) We use the preparatory object "it" to introduce an if-clause.
13 C) (= "She tried hard, but she didn't succeed...")
14 D) "As" is closest in meaning to "however" here: "Your idea is interesting, however I don't think..."
15 B) Idiomatic expression (= "I've heard it said that...")
16 D) We use the future perfect to talk about what we think will have been completed in the future.
17 A) We use "much" with uncountable nouns. "Luggage" is also an uncountable noun.
18 D) It would also be possible: "Because not only does he sing, but also..."
19 B) We use "must" + present perfect to express deduction about the past.
20 B) (= "The headlines say the mayor will resign.") "To be" + to-infinitive is used to express formality.

PART II

1 ***sooner had I arrived than***
2 ***what must be done urgently***
3 ***allowed to disqualify whoever***
4 ***saw you was a long time ago***
5 ***first time I've been***
6 ***wasn't anyone as intelligent as***
7 ***I'm looking forward to going***
8 ***had my sister answer the door***
9 ***time you left***
10 ***are bound to find***

ROUNDING OFF 4

1 a) acclimatize
b) judicious
c) lackluster
d) industrious
e) disruptive
f) demeanor
g) eligible
h) thrifty
i) dearth
j) conscientious

2 1) a 2) g 3) j 4) h 5) f 6) i 7) b 8) e 9) c 10) d

3 1) f 2) a 3) g 4) b 5) e 6) h 7) j 8) c 9) d 10) i

4 WORD FORMATION

NOUN	VERB	ADJECTIVE	ADVERB
x	x	***judicious***	judiciously
obfuscation	***obfuscate***	x	x
x	***demean***	demeaning	x
x	thrive	***thriving***	x
complacency	x	***complacent***	complacently
eligibility	x	***eligible***	x
tact	x	***tactful***	tactfully
discrepancy	x	discrepant	x
bewilderment	bewilder	***bewildering***	bewilderingly
disruption	disrupt	***disruptive***	disruptively

10 MINUTES A DAY

LESSON 21

Stage 1 Read the sentences carefully and try to figure out the meaning of the word or expression in bold from the context. Then, go on to the next Stage.

1 Europe is going through a period of ***austerity*** in order to stop the economic crisis.
2 Very young children look up to their mothers as ***paragons*** of virtue.
3 The public is now ***ostracizing*** the famous singer because of her involvement in scandals.
4 He was such a ***parsimonious*** person, but at least he's not indebted.
5 Meryl Streep is a talented woman who has ***garnered*** many awards as best actress.
6 The teacher's outstanding academic record was in fact a ***sham***.
7 The director put on a ***façade*** of self-importance to hide his insecurity.
8 When she told herself that she had lost balance during the competition, she was only trying to ***rationalize***, since she hadn't trained hard enough.
9 The politician's ***mendacious*** campaign propaganda was to be his ruin later. Voters have learned to identify defamation.
10 The waiter worked with an ***alacrity*** that pleased all the clients.

Stage 2 Match the words and expressions with their definitions or synonyms:

a) ___ [VERB]: gather, collect, accumulate
b) ___ [NOUN]: disguise, false appearance
c) ___ [VERB]: give an excuse, justify
d) ___ [ADJECTIVE]: thrifty, stingy, economical
e) ___ [ADJECTIVE]: untrue, dishonest
f) ___ [NOUN]: eagerness, willingness, quick cheerfulness
g) ___ [NOUN]: pretense, fraud, lie
h) ___ [NOUN]: models, patterns of excellence
i) ___ [VERB]: shun, reject, avoid
j) ___ [NOUN]: prudence, severity in spending

10 MINUTES A DAY

LESSON 22

Stage 1 Read the sentences carefully and try to figure out the meaning of the word or expression in bold from the context. Then, go on to the next Stage.

1 Because of the tragedy, the family sought ***solace*** in faith and friends.
2 The prisoner was an ***infamous*** man whose reputation was widely known.
3 I can't stand your ***facetious*** remarks no more. I wish you would respect my feelings.
4 It was by ***mischance*** that he lost all his fortune in gambling.
5 Poets dream about living in ***pristine*** nature, untouched by human corruption.
6 Immigrants ***delude*** themselves into believing they'll have a wonderful life in another country.
7 The professor was an ***erudite*** man who had made a name for himself while he taught at the prestigious university.
8 My mother would always ***overlook*** my mistakes when I was younger. Now my father says I'm a spoiled man.
9 The disrespectful allusion to the people's religion in the movie ***prompted*** a quick response from the audience.
10 During the interview the candidate was so nervous that she started ***fidgeting*** with the sheets of paper on the table.

Stage 2 Match the words and expressions with their definitions or synonyms:

a) ___ [VERB]: deceive, believe something that's not true
b) ___ [NOUN]: bad luck, misfortune
c) ___ [ADJECTIVE]: scholarly, learned
d) ___ [ADJECTIVE]: villainous, notorious
e) ___ [ADJECTIVE]: funny, sarcastic, inappropriate joking
f) ___ [VERB]: cause something to happen
g) ___ [NOUN]: comfort, consolation
h) ___ [VERB]: fiddle, act restlessly
i) ___ [ADJECTIVE]: intact, immaculate
j) ___ [VERB]: neglect, ignore

10 MINUTES A DAY

LESSON 23

Stage 1 Read the sentences carefully and try to figure out the meaning of the word or expression in bold from the context. Then, go on to the next Stage.

1 The research subjects were a ***random*** choice. There wasn't any previous planning.
2 You have to hand back your written ***assignments*** before the end of the term, or else your grades will be penalized.
3 The government decision ***triggered*** strong emotional responses among people.
4 I felt scared at the ***unearthly*** atmosphere surrounding the old medieval castle.
5 Everyone in the classroom looked down on the new student, but she soon ***outwitted*** them all.
6 Schools will have to ***banish*** mobile phones from classrooms.
7 Are there any ***underlying*** justifications for this project?
8 I saw the angry looking clouds in the sky as a bad ***omen***. Something terrible would follow.
9 As if she was in a trance, the woman danced with gay ***abandon***.
10 The difference between these two words is so ***subtle*** it's not worth talking about it.

Stage 2 Match the words and expressions with their definitions or synonyms:

a) ___ [VERB]: ban, eliminate
b) ___ [ADJECTIVE]: eerie, supernatural
c) ___ [ADJECTIVE]: not following a pattern or plan
d) ___ [NOUN]: recklessness, spontaneity, impulse
e) ___ [ADJECTIVE]: slight, tenuous
f) ___ [NOUN]: foreboding, augury, presage
g) ___ [VERB]: prompt, spark, cause to start
h) ___ [ADJECTIVE]: intrinsic, concealed
i) ___ [NOUN]: schoolwork, homework
j) ___ [VERB]: surpass in intelligence, outsmart

10 MINUTES A DAY

LESSON 24

Stage 1 Read the sentences carefully and try to figure out the meaning of the word or expression in bold from the context. Then, go on to the next Stage.

1 The new teacher tried in vain to ***elicit*** sympathy from the unruly students.
2 One of Shakespeare's greatest plays is being ***enacted*** at the Globe Theater.
3 Poor people around the world feel ***disenfranchised***, because their rights are blatantly ignored.
4 Either you change your ***unseemly*** behavior, or no one else will tolerate you.
5 Government authorities should work with the population's ***welfare*** in mind.
6 The child's ***irrepressible*** enthusiasm was a sure sign of a brilliant future.
7 He glanced at me ***surreptitiously***, as if trying to say something.
8 This is the most ***authoritative*** edition of this dictionary. You'll find all the information you need.
9 Archaeologists ***unveiled*** to the public a magnificent site with remains from ancient Egypt.
10 The characters try hard to ***conceal*** their true feelings to show something they are not.

Stage 2 Match the words and expressions with their definitions or synonyms:

a) ___ [VERB]: obtain, get, provoke a response
b) ___ [ADJECTIVE]: powerless, impotent, helpless
c) ___ [ADJECTIVE]: impossible to hold back, uncontrollable
d) ___ [VERB]: remove the veil, reveal
e) ___ [ADJECTIVE]: improper, inappropriate
f) ___ [VERB]: disguise, hide
g) ___ [VERB]: perform, act
h) ___ [ADJECTIVE]: trustworthy, reliable
i) ___ [NOUN]: happiness, well-being
j) ___ [ADVERB]: stealthily, hidden, secretly

10 MINUTES A DAY

LESSON 25

Stage 1 Read the sentences carefully and try to figure out the meaning of the word or expression in bold from the context. Then, go on to the next Stage.

1 The book is set against the ***backdrop*** of Victorian Age.
2 The movie is a drama about ***unrequited*** love and the fear of loneliness.
3 The challenge of producing the musical was faced with considerable ***aplomb***.
4 The play was an ***apt*** portrayal of the lifestyle of the decadent bourgeois at the end of the century.
5 He was ***doggedly*** determined to achieve all of his long-term goals.
6 His support to the project was totally committed and ***unwavering***.
7 The workers needed some ***respite*** from the tiring week.
8 He made a name for himself for his magnificent poetic ***prowess***.
9 The audience gave the actors a standing ***ovation***.
10 The actress ***stunning*** interpretation of a crazy queen earned her one more award.

Stage 2 Match the words and expressions with their definitions or synonyms:

a) ___ [ADJECTIVE]: steady, unchanging
b) ___ [ADJECTIVE]: not reciprocated
c) ___ [NOUN]: great skill, ability
d) ___ [ADJECTIVE]: surprising, shocking (in a positive way)
e) ___ [ADJECTIVE]: especially suitable, apposite
f) ___ [ADVERB]: stubbornly, determinedly
g) ___ [NOUN]: enthusiastic applause
h) ___ [NOUN]: background scenery
i) ___ [NOUN]: poise, skill, confidence
j) ___ [NOUN]: short period of rest

EXAM PRACTICE 5
GRAMMAR

Part 1 Multiple-choice

1 ___ I'd like to study more, I just don't seem to find the time.

a) while
b) when
c) meanwhile
d) however

2 Despite ___ knowing all about acupuncture, I'd still prefer traditional medicine.

a) my
b) me
c) I'm
d) I

3 "I'm not very good at Chemistry. What about you?"
"___."

a) Nor I am.
b) Nor am I.
c) Me too.
d) Not me.

4 ___ was my interest in the subject that the researcher invited me to take part in the study.

a) So
b) Much
c) Such
d) That

5 ___ more information about our program, don't hesitate to contact us.

a) You should need
b) Should you need
c) Unless you need
d) If should you need

6 ___ no wonder you've been expelled from school. You're always getting into trouble.

a) There's
b) There
c) Its
d) It's

7 An answering machine is a device ___.

a) by which your message can record
b) by which your message can be recorded
c) which message can be recorded
d) whose message can record

8 I won't ___ you, I'm sorry.
a) be able to help
b) can help
c) be capable to help
d) be able of helping

9 I am going out tonight, even if ___.
a) it rains
b) there rains
c) there's rains
d) is raining

10 What ___ lately?
a) have you doing
b) are you doing
c) have you been doing
d) have you been done

11 The heavy stones used to build the pyramids ___ by men.
a) can't have been carried
b) mustn't have been carried
c) couldn't had been carried
d) couldn't have been carrying

12 What would you like ___ done about the pollution?
a) to see
b) seeing
c) have
d) see

13 ___ I was enjoying my vacation, I was longing to come back home.
a) Much as
b) However
c) As well as
d) In spite

14 Richard was ___ any woman could dream of.

a) as polite a man
b) such man as polite
c) as polite a man as
d) so polite

15 We are going to divide the money ___ John, Robert and Sarah.

a) among
b) between
c) by
d) for

16 I'm grateful to Mrs. Vaughan, my teacher, ___ I have learned so much.

a) from whom teachings
b) from which teachings
c) whose teachings from
d) from whose teachings

17 The book ___ has been adapted to the big screen.

a) I told you about it
b) that I told you about it
c) I told you about
d) about it I told you

18 Except for some scattered showers, our holiday ___ have been better.

a) couldn't
b) could
c) may
d) mustn't

19 He got ___ furious when he realized he had been tricked.

a) very
b) absolutely
c) extremely
d) rather

20 "Which of these three movies have you seen?"
"I've seen ___."

a) neither

b) any

c) none

d) all them

Part 2 Key word transformation

Follow the same instructions as in Exam Practice 1.

1 Be careful. This bench has just been painted. **(had)**
Be careful. I ____________________________ painted.

2 Make your students read more out of classroom. **(get)**
____________________________ more out of classroom.

3 Not only is he talented but also intelligent. **(addition)**
____________________________, he is intelligent.

4 He speaks both French and Italian. **(only)**
Not ____________________________ Italian.

5 I've been working here for five years. **(ago)**
I started ____________________________.

6 I started university five years ago. **(for)**
I've ____________________________ five years.

7 They have suggested that the mayor should resign. **(been)**
It ____________________________ that the mayor should resign.

8 It appears that he has been accused of illegal practices. **(have)**
He ____________________________ of illegal practices.

9 They think he has been killed by a fan. **(thought)**
He ___________________________ by a fan.

10 It seems that there isn't any evidence against him. **(there)**
___________________________ to be any evidence against him.

ROUND OFF 5

1 Match the columns to find the antonyms of the words in bold:

1) ***austerity*** economic measures
2) ***parsimonious*** spending habits
3) ***mendacious*** statements
4) an ***erudite*** scholar
5) a ***random*** choice
6) ***banish*** mobiles from classroom
7) a ***subtle*** difference
8) people's ***welfare***
9) an ***authoritative*** encyclopedia
10) ***conceal*** your true feelings
11) an ***unrequited*** love
12) ***unwavering*** enthusiasm
13) a ***stunning*** rendition

a) ___ reveal, show
b) ___ calmness
c) ___ changeable, inconsistent

d) ___ reciprocated, returned
e) ___ lackluster, boring
f) ___ trustworthy
g) ___ ignorant
h) ___ allow, welcome, accept
i) ___ blunt, conspicuous
j) ___ prodigal, lavish
l) ___ purposive
m) ___ poverty, failure
n) ___ unreliable, untrustworthy

2 Fill in the spaces with one of these words (you may need to change some of them):

ostracize	*disenfranchised*
facetious	*unseemly*
overlook	*backdrop*
unearthly	*respite*
outwitted	*prowess*

a) Sometimes parents ___ their children's mistakes in an effort to avoid conflict.
b) The politician was being ___ by the other members of the party.
c) Many heroic narratives about knights are set against the ___ of the Middle Ages.
d) The forest ___ atmosphere made us feel a bit scarred.
e) Your petty ___, bickering argument was driving me crazy.
f) No one could stand his ___ comments during the meeting.
g) The housekeeper needed a ___ from everyday domestic drudgery.
h) The man's ___ as an orator was widely known everywhere he went.
i) The workers felt ___ by the 'government's policies, which dismissed their rights out of hand.
j) He was cleverly ___ by his opponent.

3 Match words from 1 – 10 (from exercise 2) with one of these synonyms:

a) ___ inappropriate
b) ___ flippant
c) ___ scenery
d) ___ ignore
e) ___ segregate
f) ___ uncanny
g) ___ relief
h) ___ mastery
i) ___ outsmart
j) ___ excluded

4 WORD FORMATION

NOUN	VERB	ADJECTIVE	ADVERB
austerity			
		mendacious	
	delude		
		erudite	
		subtle	
	conceal		
		stunning	
	elicit		
	banish		
		parsimonious	

Key to lessons 21 – 25

LESSON 21 – a) 5 b) 7 c) 8 d) 4 e) 9 f) 10 g) 6 h) 2 i) 3 j) 1
LESSON 22 – a) 6 b) 4 c) 7 d) 2 e) 3 f) 9 g) 1 h) 10 i) 5 j) 8
LESSON 23 – a) 6 b) 4 c) 1 d) 9 e) 10 f) 8 g) 3 h) 7 i) 2 j) 5
LESSON 24 – a) 1 b) 3 c) 6 d) 9 e) 4 f) 10 g) 2 h) 8 i) 5 j) 7
LESSON 25 – a) 6 b) 2 c) 8 d) 10 e) 4 f) 5 g) 9 h) 1 i) 3 j) 7

EXAM PRACTICE 5

PART I

1 A) (= "I'd like to study more, but I just don't seem...")
2 A) "Despite" is followed by a noun or noun phrase.
3 B) "Nor am I" is the same as "Me neither". As this is an addition to a remark, the interrogative structure (word order) is used. "Nor am I" is a formal alternative to "Me neither", which is also correct.
4 C) (= "My interest in the subject was such, that the researcher invited me...")
5 B) (= "If you should need more information...") The inversion is used to express formality.
6 D) (= "It is not surprising that you've been expelled...")
7 B) (= "... by which your message can be recorded by the caller.")
8 A) (= "It won't be possible for me to help you.")
9 A) (= "It may rain, but I will go out all the same.")
10 C) We use the present perfect simple or continuous to ask about past events which continue into the present.
11 A) We use "can (not)" + have + past participle to express deduction about the past.
12 A) (= "What would you like to see someone do about the pollution?")
13 A) (= "I did enjoy my vacation, but I was longing to come...")
14 C) In comparative structures "as...as", if we insert a noun ("man") to refer to the adjective ("polite"), the correct word order is "as + adjective + a(n) + noun + as".
15 B) We use "between", and not "among", even when we're thinking about more than two, when we think about the elements separately.
16 D) "Whose" indicates possession. "From whose teachings" = "from her teachings".
17 C) (= "... that I told you about...") We can omit the relative pronoun (underlined) when it is the object of the verb.
18 A) (= "Despite some scattered showers, our holiday was perfect.")
19 B) "Furious" is a non-gradable adjective. We use "absolutely" if we want to intensify non-gradable adjectives. (Do not use "very" / "extremely".)
20 C) (= "not any of them") Note: We use "neither" to talk about two things. "D" would be possible only if rephrased as: "I've seen all of them."

PART II

1 ***have just had this bench***
2 ***Get your students to read***
3 ***in addition to being talented***
4 ***only does he speak French but also***
5 ***working here five years ago***
6 ***been at university for***
7 ***has been suggested***
8 ***appears to have been accused***
9 ***is thought to have been killed***
10 ***There doesn't seem***

ROUNDING OFF 5

1 a) 10 b) 1 c) 12 d) 11 e) 13 f) 3 g) 4 h) 6 i) 7 j) 2 l) 5 m) 8 n) 9
2 a) overlook
b) ostracized
c) backdrop
d) uncanny
e) unseemly
f) facetious
g) respite
h) prowess
i) disenfranchised
j) outwitted
3 a) 7 b) 2 c) 8 d) 3 e) 1 f) 4 g) 9 h) 10 i) 5 j) 6
4 WORD FORMATION

NOUN	VERB	ADJECTIVE	ADVERB
austerity	x	austere	austerely
mendacity	x	***mendacious***	mendaciously
delusion	***delude***	delusional	x
erudition	x	***erudite***	eruditely
subtlety	x	***subtle***	subtly
concealment	***conceal***	x	x
x	stun	***stunning***	***stunningly***
elicitation	***elicit***	x	x
banishment	***banish***	x	x
parsimony	x	***parsimonious***	parsimoniously

10 MINUTES A DAY

LESSON 26

Stage 1 Read the sentences carefully and try to figure out the meaning of the word or expression in bold from the context. Then, go on to the next Stage.

1 I ***concede*** that your theory is interesting, but its applications are debatable.
2 I used to do ***clerical*** work at a lawyer's office as a part-time job while I attended university.
3 She achieved a ***remarkable*** nomination for the Oscar.
4 These subjects are outside my ***range***, I'm afraid. You'll have to talk to someone in authority.
5 It is possible to ***harness*** negative feelings and turn them into advantage.
6 My clothes were scattered ***haphazardly*** on the bed. I wish I were more organized.
7 You'll have to work hard to ***overcome*** your weaknesses.
8 I cannot answer this question, as it's not my ***expertise***.
9 One of the basic ***tenets*** of our theory is that everyone can learn a foreign language.
10 The driver's inexperience could seriously ***jeopardize*** our trip.

Stage 2 Match the words and expressions with their definitions or synonyms:

a) ___ [ADJECTIVE]: extraordinary, exceptional
b) ___ [ADJECTIVE]: related to office
c) ___ [NOUN]: scope, area of expertise
d) ___ [ADVERB]: casually, in a disorganized way
e) ___ [VERB]: put in danger
f) ___ [VERB]: excel, subdue, triumph
g) ___ [NOUN]: principle, basic idea
h) ___ [VERB]: admit unwillingly
i) ___ [VERB]: channel, exploit, put to use
j) ___ [NOUN]: knowledge, skill, proficiency

10 MINUTES A DAY

LESSON 27

Stage 1 Read the sentences carefully and try to figure out the meaning of the word or expression in bold from the context. Then, go on to the next Stage.

1 I was ***mesmerized*** by the breathtaking , effusive beauty of the city.
2 The ***unspeakable*** terrorist tragedy shocked the town's population.
3 She had been swimming for hours with ***stamina*** and hope in the struggle to survive.
4 Sometimes it is so hard for humans to ***endure*** the hardships of life.
5 Playing host to the Olympic Games is a ***milestone*** in the history of Brazilian sports.
6 Old, ***cumbersome*** furniture is now old fashioned.
7 The police officer was able to ***subdue*** the unruly hell-raiser.
8 The country is blessed with ***primeval*** beaches and wonderful cuisine.
9 This is a perfectly ***attainable*** objective, so I'd be more confident if I were you.
10 Doctors often take a ***dismissive*** attitude in regard to popular medicine.

Stage 2 Match the words and expressions with their definitions or synonyms:

a) ___ [ADJECTIVE]: gruesome, terrible
b) ___ [ADJECTIVE]: transfixed, marveled
c) ___ [NOUN]: an important event
d) ___ [NOUN]: resilience, energy
e) ___ [ADJECTIVE]: disdainful, contemptuous
f) ___ [VERB]: bear, put up with, tolerate
g) ___ [ADJECTIVE]: achievable, feasible
h) ___ [ADJECTIVE]: heavy, difficult to move or grasp
i) ___ [VERB]: defeat, subjugate
j) ___ [NOUN]: pristine, primordial

10 MINUTES A DAY

LESSON 28

Stage 1 Read the sentences carefully and try to figure out the meaning of the word or expression in bold from the context. Then, go on to the next Stage.

1 Finding volunteers seemed to be an ***insurmountable*** difficulty at first.
2 This medicine should be able to effectively ***counteract*** the effects of the poison.
3 When I asked what his opinion about my idea was, he only gave a ***derisive*** laugh.
4 My mother ***cajoled*** me into spending Christmas with the family.
5 Female chimpanzees are loving and caring mothers. They take due care of their ***offspring***.
6 These commercial ads are sure to ***entice*** you to buy things you didn't even know existed.
7 She wasn't a brilliant student at school. She would always get ***mediocre*** grades.
8 The children were ***enthralled*** by the merry-go-round colorful horses.
9 My father has had an ***entrepreneurship*** flair since he was very young.
10 His heart was ***devoid*** of any compassion towards others.

Stage 2 Match the words and expressions with their definitions or synonyms:

a) ___ [ADJECTIVE]: contemptuous, disdainful
b) ___ [ADJECTIVE]: of average, second rate quality
c) ___ [ADJECTIVE]: hypnotized, fascinated
d) ___ [NOUN]: a person's children or an animal's young
e) ___ [ADJECTIVE]: insuperable
f) ___ [VERB]: persuade, talk someone into doing something
g) ___ [ADJECTIVE]: bereft of, empty
h) ___ [VERB]: lure, persuade
i) ___ [VERB]: fight, produce the opposite effect
j) ___ [NOUN]: business skill

10 MINUTES A DAY

LESSON 29

Stage 1 Read the sentences carefully and try to figure out the meaning of the word or expression in bold from the context. Then, go on to the next Stage.

1 She had an ***unassertive*** tone of voice which was a disadvantage to her as a boss.
2 No one was able to call into question his ***adamant*** resolutions.
3 I didn't like him as a partner at work because he was so ***nonchalant*** about everything.
4 My sister's ***homely*** style meant she wasn't very popular among boys at school.
5 They were a crowd of ***boisterous*** boys, but they were lovely anyway.
6 The accident boiled down to a ***perfunctory*** inspection of the plane.
7 The money was illegal, but it was processed through ***laundering***.
8 He was a brilliant teacher whose talent ***surpassed*** everyone at school.
9 My mind was ***teeming*** with ideas, so I had to sit down and write a draft.
10 If I were you, I'd ***give myself up***. There's no way out.

Stage 2 Match the words and expressions with their definitions or synonyms:

a) _ _ _ [ADJECTIVE]: bland, unattractive
b) _ _ _ [VERB]: surrender
c) _ _ _ [ADJECTIVE]: submissive, unconvincing
d) _ _ _ [NOUN]: washing (figuratively)
e) _ _ _ [ADJECTIVE]: firmly determined
f) _ _ _ [VERB]: exceed
g) _ _ _ [ADJECTIVE]: full of
h) _ _ _ [VERB]: cool, carefree, casual
i) _ _ _ [ADJECTIVE]: superficial, cursory
j) _ _ _ [ADJECTIVE]: rambunctious, lively, energetic

10 MINUTES A DAY

LESSON 30

Stage 1 Read the sentences carefully and try to figure out the meaning of the word or expression in bold from the context. Then, go on to the next Stage.

1 The teacher gave only a ***non-committal*** answer when asked what her opinion was.
2 People are fed up with that politicians' ***nonsensical*** promises.
3 My son works with ***diligence*** in order to achieve his objectives.
4 Corruption among politicians in this state is ***rampant***.
5 They held the eminent architect's ***wake*** at the presidential palace.
6 The pursuit of excellence is a ***hallmark*** of this prestigious institution.
7 Love towards humanity is one of the ***cornerstones*** of our religion.
8 This product has achieved ***iconic*** status through advertising.
9 These hotels may look ***unprepossessing*** at a first glance, but they offer first-class service.
10 I wish you would stop ***bragging*** about your personal achievements.

Stage 2 Match the words and expressions with their definitions or synonyms:

a) ___ [ADJECTIVE]: the fundamental reason for the existence of something
b) ___ [VERB]: swagger, boast
c) ___ [NOUN]: watch held over a dead person's body
d) ___ [NOUN]: a distinguishing feature
e) ___ [ADJECTIVE]: evasive, restrained, trying to hide your opinion
f) ___ [ADJECTIVE]: very common, widespread
g) ___ [ADJECTIVE]: homely, bland, unattractive
h) ___ [ADJECTIVE]: absurd, stupid
i) ___ [NOUN]: serious application to a pursuit
j) ___ [ADJECTIVE]: an impressive symbol of something

EXAM PRACTICE 6
GRAMMAR

Part 1 Multiple-choice

1 ___ you should need further information, just let us know.

a) If
b) When
c) Whenever
d) Unless

2 He had already tried many different kinds of treatment. ___, he hardly showed any sign of recovery.

a) Even though
b) Yet
c) Whereas
d) Nevertheless

3 I don't think it's worth ___ in this project.

a) to take

b) that we take

c) taking

d) we take

4 "Do you think Mark will resign?"
"I ___."

a) suppose not

b) don't suppose it

c) think it so

d) don't suppose

5 When the police arrived, the thieves ___.

a) already escaped

b) had escaped already

c) had already escaped

d) had already been escaped

6 I want to study French ___ Italian.

a) but also

b) as well

c) and as well

d) as well as

7 ___ must have been an accident. They should have already shown up.

a) There

b) It

c) They

d) There's

8 When I arrived at school, I realized it was Saturday. I ___.

a) didn't need to go

b) needn't have gone

c) needn't go
d) needn't had gone

9 ___ these irrelevant mistakes, your composition is well written.
a) Alongside
b) Except
c) Apart from
d) As well as

10 ___ mum prepared lunch, we would play happily in the yard when we were children.
a) While
b) Meanwhile
c) Then
d) Unless

11 You ___ have told me what you intended to do. Now you've ruined everything.
a) must
b) might
c) may
d) had to

12 Do you remember ___ this movie before?
a) to have seen
b) you had seen
c) having seen
d) have seen

13 ___ good as it seems to be, I still feel you should improve your paper.
a) So
b) As
c) However
d) Though

14 The teacher demanded that he ___ in his homework.
a) handing
b) is handing
c) would hand
d) hand

15 I ___ hope to see you again.
a) do
b) not
c) am
d) want

16 I wish you hadn't done anything about it without ___ to me first.
a) talk
b) you had talked
c) you talked
d) talking

17 I was ___ terrified by the news.
a) utterly
b) very
c) deeply
d) much

18 "Ron said he has given up the course."
"It ___ . He didn't have much time to study and work."
a) was well done
b) might as well
c) serves him right
d) was just as well

19 ___ ten percent of the candidates actually turned up.
a) fewer than
b) less than

c) as fewer as
d) as much as

20 The task was so easy that ___ a child could have done it.
a) even
b) still
c) until
d) despite

Part 2 Key word transformation

Follow the same instructions as in Exam Practice 1.

1 There is a rumor that the criminal is living abroad. **(rumored)**
The criminal ____________________________ abroad.

2 Burglars broke into our car last night. **(got)**
Our car ____________________________ by burglars last night.

3 If you are here by any chance, pay me a visit. **(happen)**
If you ____________________________, pay me a visit.

4 I wouldn't have been successful if you hadn't helped me. **(but)**
____________________________, I wouldn't have been successful.

5 You are sick now because you ate too much. **(if)**
____________________________ too much, you wouldn't be sick now.

6 You shouldn't stay up late. **(rather)**
I'd ____________________________ late.

7 I'd rather you didn't say anything about that. **(prefer)**
I'd ____________________________ anything about that.

8 Our relationship is not very good. **(along)**
We ___________________________ with each other.

9 Would you like to go for a walk? **(up)**
Do you feel ___________________________ for a walk?

10 The woman cried when she heard the news. **(broke)**
The woman ___________________________ she heard the news.

ROUND OFF 6

1 Match sentences 1 – 10 to replace the words (or expressions) underlined with a synonym (A – J):

1) We should try to ***control*** these negative feelings and build something positive instead.
2) The ski instructor's inability ***put*** our adventure ***in danger***.
3) When I was introduced to her, she gave me a ***disdainful*** handshake.
4) I was ***hypnotized*** by the breathtaking beauty of the blue ocean waters.
5) My boss answered my question with a ***contemptuous*** laugh.
6) The student ***persuaded*** his teacher to accept his belated homework.
7) The young executive, having no work experience, was still ***insecure*** and self-conscious.
8) The car broke down because of the ***superficial*** inspection.
9) Efficiency is ***of basic importance*** to our company's success.
10) These ***plain looking*** museums are home to the most important works of art.

a) ___ cajole
b) ___ cornerstone
c) ___ derisive

d) ___ dismissive
e) ___ harness
f) ___ jeopardize
g) ___ mesmerized
h) ___ perfunctory
i) ___ unassertive
j) ___ unprepossessing

2 Match the words underlined with their synonyms or definitions:

1) The clothes were thrown haphazardly all over the bedroom.
2) Among the basic tenets of this company, the most important should be equal treatment.
3) The demonstrations all over the country were hailed as a milestone in the fight against corruption.
4) All men have a primeval desire to subdue their rivals.
5) Modern circuses are working hard to entice a new public into the spectacles.
6) She lacked confidence because she regarded herself as homely and stupid.
7) The club was full of boisterous teenagers bragging about their skills.
8) The witness tried to answer the judge's questions in a noncommittal tone.
9) Professionalism and competence are a hallmark of our commitment to quality in education.
10) Da Vinci has enjoyed iconic status for his painting.

a) ___ principles
b) ___ primordial
c) ___ sprightly
d) ___ unattractive
e) ___ emblematic
f) ___ disorderly
g) ___ reticent
h) ___ characteristic
i) ___ allure
j) ___ signpost

3 Match the following words with an antonym:

haphazard	*entice*
primeval	*boisterous*
homely	*non-committal*

a) ___ definitely
b) ___ thought-out
c) ___ beautiful
d) ___ dissuade
e) ___ restrained
f) ___ modern

4 WORD FORMATION

NOUN	VERB	ADJECTIVE	ADVERB
	concede		
		remarkable	
	jeopardize		
	attain		
		dismissive	
		derisive	
	entice		
		mediocre	
diligence			
		(un) assertive	

Key to lessons 26 – 30

LESSON 26 – a) 3 b) 2 c) 4 d) 6 e) 10 f) 7 g) 9 h) 1 i) 5 j) 8
LESSON 27 – a) 2 b) 1 c) 5 d) 3 e) 10 f) 4 g) 9 h) 6 i) 7 j) 8
LESSON 28 – a) 3 b) 7 c) 8 d) 5 e) 1 f) 4 g) 10 h) 6 i) 2 j) 9
LESSON 29 – a) 4 b) 10 c) 1 d) 7 e) 2 f) 8 g) 9 h) 3 i) 6 j) 5
LESSON 30 – a) 7 b) 10 c) 5 d) 6 e) 1 f) 4 g) 9 h) 2 i) 3 j) 8

EXAM PRACTICE 6

PART I

1 A) (= "If you need any help...") Formal usage. Another option is "Should you need further..."
2 D) (= however)
3 C) The phrase "it's worth", if followed by a verb, always take the gerund. (Note that "worth" is a preposition.)
4 A) "I don't suppose so" would also be possible.
5 C) We insert adverbs after the first auxiliary ("had already escaped").
6 D) (= "I want to study French and Italian.") It would also be possible: "I want to study French and Italian as well."
7 A) "There" here acts as a "preparatory subject".
8 B) "Needn't have" + participle means that it wasn't necessary, but I did it.
9 C) (= "to the exception of")
10 A) Attention to letter B: "Meanwhile" cannot be used to introduce the first sentence.
11 B) We use "might" to express strong criticism about the past. It is close in meaning to "You should have told..."
12 C) The verb "remember" is followed by the gerund to refer to the past. "Do you remember seeing this movie before" would also be possible.
13 B) (= "However good it seems to be, I still think...")
14 D) We use the bare infinitive in the subjunctive (American English). In British English, "should" is normally used: "The teacher demanded that he (should) hand in..." In less formal contexts, especially in British English, "The teacher demanded that he hands / handed..." would also be possible.
15 A) We can use the auxiliary "do" in an affirmative sentence to make it more emphatic.
16 D) After prepositions, verbs always take the gerund form.
17 A) We use "utterly" (or "absolutely") to intensify a non-gradable adjective. "Extremely" and "very" cannot be used in this case.
18 D) (= "He did the right thing, as there wasn't anything else to do.")

19 A) "Fewer" is used to refer to the countable noun "candidates". "Less" is widely used before plural countable nouns in informal style.
20 A) (= "Although you might not expect a child to be able to do this, a child can do it.")

PART II

1 ***is rumored to be living***
2 ***got broken into***
3 ***happen to be here***
4 ***But for your help***
5 ***If you hadn't eaten***
6 ***rather you didn't stay up***
7 ***prefer it if you didn't say***
8 ***don't get along well***
9 ***up to going***
10 ***broke down when*** (or: ***broke into tears)***

ROUNDING OFF 6

1 a) 6 b) 9 c) 5 d) 3 e) 1 f) 2 g) 4 h) 8 i) 7 j) 10
2 a) 2 b) 4 c) 7 d) 6 e) 10 f) 1 g) 8 h) 9 i) 5 j) 3
3 a) 6 b) 1 c) 3 d) 4 e) 5 f) 2
4 WORD FORMATION

NOUN	VERB	ADJECTIVE	ADVERB
concession	***concede***	x	x
x	remark	***remarkable***	remarkably
jeopardy	***jeopardize***	x	x
attainment	***attain***	attainable	x
dismissal	dismiss	***dismissive***	dismissively
derision	deride	***derisive***	derisively
enticement	***entice***	enticing	enticingly
mediocrity	x	***mediocre***	x
diligence	x	diligent	diligently
(un) assertiveness	assert	***(un) assertive***	(un) assertively

10 MINUTES A DAY

LESSON 31

Stage 1 Read the sentences carefully and try to figure out the meaning of the word or expression in bold from the context. Then, go on to the next Stage.

1 The small company's ***takeover*** by a bigger one came as a surprise to investors.
2 He ***renounced*** his candidacy for mayor of the city because of scandals.
3 Virtual relationship on the internet is having a ***deleterious*** effect on people's perceptions of friendship.
4 It is necessary to do something to ***defuse*** the tense climate among strikers.
5 I had this ***exhilarating*** feeling you get when you achieve something big.
6 The student ended up getting a fail grade because of ***plagiarism***.
7 The critics wrote ***effusive*** reviews to promote the writer's new book.
8 Political unrest is ***begetting*** a tense climate of war.
9 The young racer met his ***untimely*** death in a competition.
10 The city's skyline was a beauty to ***behold***.

Stage 2 Match the words and expressions with their definitions or synonyms:

a) ___ [ADJECTIVE]: pernicious, harmful
b) ___ [NOUN]: use someone else's ideas as if they were your own
c) ___ [VERB]: calm, placate
d) ___ [NOUN]: merge, incorporation
e) ___ [ADJECTIVE]: unreservedly enthusiastic
f) ___ [ADJECTIVE]: exciting, stimulating
g) ___ [VERB]: give up
h) ___ [ADJECTIVE]: premature, earlier than expected
i) ___ [VERB]: see
j) ___ [VERB]: bring about, promote

10 MINUTES A DAY

LESSON 32

Stage 1 Read the sentences carefully and try to figure out the meaning of the word or expression in bold from the context. Then, go on to the next Stage.

1 The politician was convicted of ***embezzlement*** in a millionaire corruption scheme.
2 The scandal was a terrible ***setback*** in that famous singer's career.
3 This university doesn't ***endorse*** publications of preparatory materials by other universities.
4 After lying before the judge in court he was feeling ***remorseful***.
5 The prosecutor's ***compelling*** arguments convinced the jury.
6 This short story ***embodies*** the struggle of women for emancipation.
7 He was a loner, with his ***withdrawn*** personality.
8 The group was planning an excursion through the ***untamed*** Amazon's forests.
9 You'll have to ***hustle***, or else you will miss your plane.
10 The enchanting monument known as Taj Mahal became a famous ***landmark*** in India.

Stage 2 Match the words and expressions with their definitions or synonyms:

a) ___ [ADJECTIVE]: guilty, sorry for something you regret having done
b) ___ [NOUN]: a point of reference
c) ___ [VERB]: represent, be a symbol of
d) ___ [NOUN]: something that hinders progress, an obstacle, a hindrance
e) ___ [ADJECTIVE]: wild, in its original state, pristine
f) ___ [ADJECTIVE]: aloof, distant, solitary
g) ___ [VERB]: express support publicly or officially
h) ___ [VERB]: move quickly
i) ___ [NOUN]: theft, appropriation (of money you've been trusted with)
j) ___ [ADJECTIVE]: capable of making someone believe in something, convincing

10 MINUTES A DAY

LESSON 33

Stage 1 Read the sentences carefully and try to figure out the meaning of the word or expression in bold from the context. Then, go on to the next Stage.

1 People suspected he was involved in corruption because he lived an ***ostentatious*** life.
2 Tourists come from all over the world to watch the carnival ***floats*** parade.
3 This family ***feud*** has been going on for decades on end.
4 I wish you'd stop behaving like a ***hedonist***. There's more to life than pleasure.
5 The athlete received the news of his victory with tears of ***mirth***.
6 Rio de Janeiro boasts a Christmas three lavishly ***festooned*** with a myriad of lights.
7 The criminal was on ***parole*** when he decided to commit the crime.
8 She always ***gorges*** herself on chocolate. She's addicted to it.
9 The terrorist leader was caught by the soldiers after being under ***surveillance*** for months.
10 The resignation of the political leader brought about dreadful ***mayhem***.

Stage 2 Match the words and expressions with their definitions or synonyms:

a) ___ [NOUN]: someone who is always seeking pleasure
b) ___ [NOUN]: careful watch scheme
c) ___ [VERB]: eat greedily
d) ___ [ADJECTIVE]: showy, extravagant, pompous
e) ___ [NOUN]: gaiety, cheerfulness, hilarity
f) ___ [NOUN]: chaos, disorder
g) ___ [ADJECTIVE]: bedecked, adorned, decorated
h) ___ [NOUN]: procession trucks on which people dance
i) ___ [NOUN]: release a prisoner before the official end of his sentence
j) ___ [NOUN]: vendetta, quarrel

10 MINUTES A DAY

LESSON 34

Stage 1 Read the sentences carefully and try to figure out the meaning of the word or expression in bold from the context. Then, go on to the next Stage.

1 This machine will ***enable*** workers to produce more in less time.
2 The difficulties you have to deal with are ***inherent*** to the work.
3 The mayor made a ***robust*** defense of his governmental policies.
4 ***Unbeknown*** to parents, may children start taking drugs at school.
5 These allergies are attributed to ***airborne*** pollutants like pollen.
6 The boy looked at his teacher with a ***roguish*** smile on his face.
7 Your achievements in the field of medicine research are ***laudable***.
8 The principal ***rebuked*** the teachers for not working hard enough.
9 Sometimes I like to ***pamper*** myself with luxurious things.
10 Teachers tend to be more ***permissive*** nowadays than in the past.

Stage 2 Match the words and expressions with their definitions or synonyms:

a) ___ [VERB]: allow, permit, give someone the means to do something
b) ___ [VERB]: scold, tell off, reprimand
c) ___ [ADJECTIVE]: praiseworthy, commendable
d) ___ [ADJECTIVE]: tolerant (slightly negative connotation)
e) ___ [ADJECTIVE]: powerful, convincing, forcefully expressed (figurative)
f) ___ [ADJECTIVE]: carried by air
g) ___ [ADJECTIVE]: mischievous, about to behave badly
h) ___ [ADJECTIVE]: intrinsic, a natural part of
i) ___ [VERB]: to treat yourself or others indulgently
j) ___ [ADJECTIVE]: unaware of

10 MINUTES A DAY

LESSON 35

Stage 1 Read the sentences carefully and try to figure out the meaning of the word or expression in bold from the context. Then, go on to the next Stage.

1 The exam results have been ***postponed*** until a later date.
2 In a ***peremptory*** tone of voice, she told us to leave immediately.
3 After my wife's death, I tried hard to live through the ***morass*** of depression.
4 The journalist was punished for ***purveying*** sensationalist news and gossip.
5 The boss was an intimidating person. He had a ***redoubtable*** character.
6 It was on a ***lugubrious*** night that she committed suicide.
7 He was so ***avid*** for money that he was thought to be involved in embezzlement.
8 The athlete was sweating ***profusely*** when he completed the task.
9 She was ***unabashed*** by her faults because she was making efforts to improve.
10 He was an admirable person for being a ***keen*** worker.

Stage 2 Match the words and expressions with their definitions or synonyms:

a) ___ [VERB]: transmit
b) ___ [VERB]: delay, put off
c) ___ [ADJECTIVE]: not embarrassed, ashamed or shy
d) ___ [ADJECTIVE]: enthusiastic
e) ___ [ADJECTIVE]: gloomy, melancholic, sad
f) ___ [ADJECTIVE]: imperious, domineering
g) ___ [ADJECTIVE]: powerful, strong (in an unfriendly, impolite way)
h) ___ [ADJECTIVE]: a keen interest in something, eager
i) ___ [NOUN]: quagmire, a situation which does not improve
j) ___ [ADVERB]: in large amounts

EXAM PRACTICE 7
GRAMMAR

Part 1 Multiple-choice

1 ___ your students write a composition every class.

a) do

b) get

c) have

d) tell

2 I'm looking forward to ___ to Europe.

a) travel

b) traveling

c) my traveling

d) me traveling

3 It's much too late. It's high time ___ home.

a) to go

b) I go

c) I should go

d) I went

4 I ___ in this company since I moved here ten years ago.

a) have worked

b) am working

c) would work

d) work

5 My wife left her teaching job, ___.

a) as was my mother

b) like did my mother

c) and so was my mother

d) as did my mother

6 Mary works ___ a secretary at a language institute.

a) like

b) as

c) how

d) alike

7 This test isn't ___ the one we did last semester.

a) nearly as hard as

b) so hard

c) nearly as hard

d) just hard as

8 I would have lent you the money if I ___ you needed.

a) know

b) knew

c) had known
d) known

9 If I ___ you, I wouldn't talk back to your mother. It's disrespectful.
a) were
b) should be
c) would be
d) was

10 What I'd like to know is what ___ if you had been in my place.
a) would you do
b) would you have done
c) you would had
d) you would have done

11 The new employee was dismissed because he ___ money.
a) was seen stealing
b) was seen stolen
c) had seen stolen
d) had seen stealing

12 The family had their house ___ into last night.
a) to break
b) to be broken
c) breaking
d) broken

13 You look drained! You ___ have been working all day.
a) might
b) may
c) could
d) must

14 ___ done all my homework, I went to a friend's house.

a) Having
b) Have
c) To have
d) I have

15 John plays the piano very well, and so ___ his wife.

a) plays
b) does
c) is
d) can

16 I'd advise you to study hard ___ a high pass grade.

a) for you getting
b) for you you get
c) so that you get
d) so as to getting

17 The teacher proved himself to be incapable ___ with adolescents.

a) to work
b) of working
c) to working
d) at working

18 ___ so much unemployment, the young people are leaving the country.

a) With
c) As with
c) For being
d) As for

19 ___ being no more objections, the president approved the project immediately.

a) It
b) It is

c) There's
d) There

20 Scarcely had I sat down ___ the movie started.
a) when
b) than
c) then
d) so

Part 2 Key word transformation

Follow the same instructions as in Exam Practice 1.

1 I accidentally met Jim at the party. **(into)**
I ____________________________ at the party.

2 The doctor told him to quit smoking. **(advised)**
The doctor ____________________________ smoking.

3 I'm looking forward to travelling overseas. **(dying)**
____________________________ overseas.

4 It appears that there are some complaints about him. **(there)**
____________________________ some complaints about him.

5 It's useless to cry over spilled milk. **(point)**
There's ____________________________ over spilled milk.

6 I will do what I've planned, no matter what happens. **(through)**
I will ____________________________ my plans, no matter what happens.

7 The doctor didn't expect the patient to survive. **(pull)**
The doctor didn't expect the patient ____________________________.

8 I prefer reading a book to watching a movie. **(sooner)**
I ___________________________ a movie.

9 I want to get rid of the job interview soon. **(over)**
I want to get ___________________________ soon.

10 I haven't been able to write my thesis yet. **(succeed)**
I ___________________________ my thesis yet.

ROUND OFF 7

1 Fill in the blanks with one of the following words or expressions:

deleterious	***withdrawn***
defuse	***feud***
untimely	***mayhem***
setback	***unbeknown***
compelling	***permissive***

a) The politician's involvement in a sexual scandal was a ___ in his campaign. ***(a problem that prevents progress)***

b) The student's spoiled character had a ___ effect among the other students in class. ***(damaging, harmful)***

c) This family ___ has been going on for generations and many people have died as a result. ***(quarrel, fight)***

d) The irate mob brought about ___ to the city center last night during the protests. ***(chaos)***

e) People all over the country expressed their sadness for the rock singer's ___ death. ***(happening too early)***

f) In today's ___ society, it is difficult for parents to get their teachings across to children. ***(not strict, too flexible)***

g) ___ to the teacher, the students had copied their schoolwork from the Internet. ***(without knowing)***

h) It was necessary to do something to ___ the tense climate in the company after a worker was dismissed. ***(improve a bad situation)***

i) There was ___ evidence for the jury to reach a consensus. ***(convincing)***

j) The boy was an abashed, ___ student who was always alienating people. ***(shy, quiet)***

2 Match the two halves:

a) violence ... more violence

b) an incredible site to ...

c) send a politician to prison for ...

d) one of the country's most famous ...

e) the nightclub was under ...

f) to have a ..., attractive smile

g) your merits are ...

h) ... yourself with some presents

i) to ... an examination

j) to have to follow ... instructions

k) to face a ... rival

l) to offer someone ... support

1) ___ behold

2) ___ surveillance

3) ___ laudable

4) ___ pamper

5) ___ embezzlement

6) ___ postpone

7) ___ peremptory

8) ___ begets

9) ___ unabashed

10) ___ roguish

11) ___ redoubtable
12) ___ landmarks

3 Match the words 1 – 12 (from exercise 2) with these synonyms:

a) ___ dictatorially
b) ___ see
c) ___ malversation
d) ___marker
e) ___ shameless
f) ___ watching
g) ___ awe inspiring
h) ___ indulge
i) ___ delay
j) ___ praiseworthy
k) ___ naughty
l) ___ bring about

4 WORD FORMATION

NOUN	VERB	ADJECTIVE	ADVERB
		exhilarating	
		ostentatious	
		permissive	
	postpone		
			profusely
		keen	
		avid	
		laudable	
		roguish	
		remorseful	

Key to lessons 31-35

LESSON 31 – a) 3 b) 6 c) 4 d) 1 e) 7 f) 5 g) 2 h) 9 i) 10 j) 8
LESSON 32 – a) 4 b) 10 c) 6 d) 2 e) 8 f) 7 g) 3 h) 9 i) 1 j) 5
LESSON 33 – a) 4 b) 9 c) 8 d) 1 e) 5 f) 10 g) 6 h) 2 i) 7 j) 3
LESSON 34 – a) 1 b) 8 c) 7 d) 10 e) 3 f) 5 g) 6 h) 2 i) 9 j) 4
LESSON 35 – a) 4 b) 1 c) 9 d) 10 e) 6 f) 2 g) 5 h) 7 i) 3 j) 8

EXAM PRACTICE 7

PART I

1 C) "Have your students write a composition..." means the same as "Make your students write...". The pattern in A is never possible (compare: "You can't make me do this."); B would be possible if rephrased as "Get your students to write..." (with a slight difference in meaning). For more on this, check a grammar book for the use of "causative verbs".

2 B) In the phrase "look forward to", "to" is a preposition, therefore it is always followed by the gerund.

3 D) Fixed expression. "It's time (for me) to go" would also be possible.

4 A) We use the present perfect to talk about something that started in the past and continues into the present. "Since" is used to indicate when something started.

5 D) That is, "My mother left her teaching job too". You might encounter examples of usage as as in B, but this is not regarded as correct by the standard.

6 B) Be careful: "Mary works like a dog" would only be a comparison. She isn't a dog.

7 A) That is, "The test we did last semester was much harder than this test."

8 C) We use the past perfect ("had known") in the if-clause when the main clause is introduced by the perfect conditional: "I would have lent..."

9 A) Please note: "If I was", even though current, is informal.

10 D) Please note that this is an indirect question. Therefore, you cannot use the interrogative structure pattern (inversion of subject and verb).

11 A) (= "Someone saw him stealing.") Check for passive and active voices.

12 D) (= "Someone broke into the family's house last night.")

13 D) We use "must" to express strong speculation about the past.

14 A) (= "After I had done all my work, I went to...")

15 B) (= "and his wife does too")

16 C) (= "... hard, in order for you to get...") D would be possible if rephrased as: "so as to get", but this is formal.

17 B) Adjective pattern. "Incapable" is always followed by "of".

18 A) (= "Because there is so much...")
19 D) "There" acts as a "preparatory subject" here.
20 B) The phrase "Scarcely / no sooner had L.." is followed by another clause beginning with "than".

PART II

1. ***ran into Jim***
2. ***advised that he (should) quit***
3. ***I'm dying to travel***
4. ***There appears to be***
5. ***no point inin crying***
6. ***go through with***
7. ***to pull through (OR: would pull through)***
8. ***would sooner read a book than watch***
9. ***the job interview over with***
10. ***didn't succeed in writing***

ROUNDING OFF 7

1. a) setback b) deleterious c) feud d) mayhem e) untimely f) permissive g) unbeknown h) defuse i) compelling j) withdrawn
2. 1) b 2) e 3) g 4) h 5) c 6) i 7) j 8) a 9) l 10) f 11) k 12) d
3. a) 7 b) 1 c) 5 d) 12 e) 9 f) 2 g) 11 h) 4 i) 6 j) 3 k) 10 l) 8
4. WORD FORMATION

NOUN	VERB	ADJECTIVE	ADVERB
exhilaration	exhilarate	***exhilarating***	x
ostentation	x	***ostentatious***	ostentatiously
permissiveness	x	***permissive***	x
postponement	***postpone***	x	x
profusion, profuseness	x	***profuse***	***profusely***
keenness	x	***keen***	keenly
x	x	***avid***	avidly
x	laud	***laudable***	laudably
x	x	***roguish***	roguishly
remorse	x	***remorseful***	remorsefully

10 MINUTES A DAY

LESSON 36

Stage 1 Read the sentences carefully and try to figure out the meaning of the word or expression in bold from the context. Then, go on to the next Stage.

1 The teacher said she didn't want to ***resort*** to any kind of harsh punishment.
2 You're only pretending to be a ***righteous*** person to have people's admiration.
3 What I liked best about the service was that everyone was very ***accommodating***.
4 The hotel service was rather ***shoddy***, that's why I canceled my reservation.
5 There was a ***backlog*** of documents for me to sign when I returned to work.
6 My new cell phone is under ***warranty***, so I'll have it fixed by the support.
7 Prices have been so ***erratic*** lately because of the inflation.
8 The proud teacher ***extolled*** the virtues of her devoted students.
9 No one knows what could possibly ***account for*** the mistakes made by that competent professional.
10 As a competent journalist, you have to keep ***abreast*** of the latest news.

Stage 2 Match the words and expressions with their definitions or synonyms:

a) ___ [VERB]: explain, justify
b) ___ [VERB]: laud, praise highly
c) ___ [ADJECTIVE]: shabby, done carelessly
d) ___ [NOUN]: guarantee
e) ___ [ADJECTIVE]: acquainted, informed
f) ___ [ADJECTIVE]: helpful, friendly, considerate
g) ___ [VERB]: make use of something reluctantly
h) ___ [ADJECTIVE]: upright, virtuous, morally good
i) ___ [NOUN]: a stockpile of uncompleted work
j) ___ [ADJECTIVE]: irregular, changeable

10 MINUTES A DAY

LESSON 37

Stage 1 Read the sentences carefully and try to figure out the meaning of the word or expression in bold from the context. Then, go on to the next Stage.

1 Having a certificate of proficiency in English can be an ***asset*** to your career.
2 Classical music is so beautiful and ***atmospheric***.
3 Catholics are encouraged not to eat meat as a ***penance*** for Lent.
4 A ***raucous*** crowd gathered in front of the presidential residence.
5 The judge has ***abrogated*** the law which banned gays from the army.
6 Immigrants go to the United States every year seeking ***asylum*** and opportunities.
7 The Jewish are ***persecuted*** all over the world for their religious beliefs.
8 The judge gave the accused a ***withering*** look, which made him feel scorned.
9 Mastering a foreign language is a ***gateway*** to a successful career.
10 The problem with the movie is that it is fraught with ***unsettling*** images.

Stage 2 Match the words and expressions with their definitions or synonyms:

a) ___ [VERB]: abolish, reject, cancel
b) ___ [NOUN]: shelter, cover, protection
c) ___ [ADJECTIVE]: which helps to create a pleasant feeling
d) ___ [NOUN]: aid, benefit
e) ___ [ADJECTIVE]: loud, harsh noise
f) ___ [VERB]: harass, bother, pester
g) ___ [NOUN]: access, entrance
h) ___ [ADJECTIVE]: disconcerting, disturbing
i) ___ [NOUN]: punishment, penitence
j) ___ [ADJECTIVE]: shrink, wane (figuratively: which makes someone feel ignored)

10 MINUTES A DAY

LESSON 38

Stage 1 Read the sentences carefully and try to figure out the meaning of the word or expression in bold from the context. Then, go on to the next Stage.

1 This pianist always gives ***dazzling*** performances which blind the audience.
2 Our mayor is a ***philistine*** man who refuses to invest in art or culture.
3 Some brands like Coca Cola have become ***household*** names .
4 His declarations were seen as ***tantamount*** to irresponsible accusations.
5 You're doing yourself a ***disservice*** by trying to be on good terms with him.
6 The criminal's house was ***besieged*** by heavily armed police officers.
7 Passengers aboard the ship saw the incident as a ***foreshadowing*** of ominous things to come.
8 A pack of ***ravenous*** animals died at the zoo for lack of food and proper caring.
9 The scientist ***cogently*** argued that it is necessary to employ animals in research.
10 Rio de Janeiro has a ***beguiling*** charm that attracts visitors from all over the world.

Stage 2 Match the words and expressions with their definitions or synonyms:

a) ___ **[VERB]**: surround and blockade a place in order to capture
b) ___ **[ADJECTIVE]**: stunning, very impressive
c) ___ **[ADVERB]**: convincingly
d) ___ **[ADJECTIVE]**: enticing, captivating, charming
e) ___ **[NOUN]**: unhelpful, harmful action
f) ___ **[ADJECTIVE]**: widely known, established, popular
g) ___ **[ADJECTIVE]**: extremely hungry
h) ___ **[NOUN]**: foreboding, presage, an advance sign of something
i) ___ **[ADJECTIVE]**: someone who's unable to appreciate the value of art or culture
j) ___ **[ADJECTIVE]**: equivalent

10 MINUTES A DAY

LESSON 39

Stage 1 Read the sentences carefully and try to figure out the meaning of the word or expression in bold from the context. Then, go on to the next Stage.

1. The politician devoted his life to fighting religious ***bigotry***.
2. They were a bundle of ***fractious*** teenagers who were always causing trouble at school.
3. The religious leader was a mean man with some ***nefarious*** purposes hidden behind his false appearance.
4. If you want to achieve academic success, excellence is seen as ***paramount*** at our school.
5. When in pursuit of your objectives, don't ***falter*** in your resolve. Keep making efforts.
6. The protesters hurled ***invective*** against the politician.
7. Even though my boss was a wealthy man, he wore ***nondescript*** clothes lacking in elegance.
8. The vacationers wanted an ***idyllic*** weekend far from the city's hustle and bustle.
9. The teacher ***reproached*** us severely because we hadn't done our homework.
10. He over-indulged himself in a life of ***debauchery*** and madness.

Stage 2 Match the words and expressions with their definitions or synonyms:

a) ___ [ADJECTIVE]: of utmost importance
b) ___ [ADJECTIVE]: common, ordinary
c) ___ [NOUN]: bias, prejudice, intolerance
d) ___ [VERB]: rebuke, reprimand
e) ___ (***adjective***): wicked, criminal
f) ___ [VERB]: hesitate, lose confidence or enthusiasm
g) ___ [NOUN]: revelry, depravity
h) ___ [ADJECTIVE]: peaceful and happy
i) ___ [ADJECTIVE]: irritable, hard to control
j) ___ [NOUN]: insulting, offensive verbal abuse

10 MINUTES A DAY

LESSON 40

Stage 1 Read the sentences carefully and try to figure out the meaning of the word or expression in bold from the context. Then, go on to the next Stage.

1 You are so ***naive***. How can you believe what Henry says?
2 It was a ***felicitous*** coincidence to run into my cousin at the party.
3 Teachers need to create an atmosphere in classroom which is ***conducive*** to learning.
4 This chapter ***recapitulates*** some of the points we've covered before.
5 He was so tired of carrying his ***unwieldy*** suitcase everywhere he went.
6 Society expects everyone to conform to the commonly accepted ***propriety***.
7 His paintings are a true example of resourceful ***artifice***.
8 Besides being very soft spoken and polite, she was a ***comely*** woman.
9 India and China are ***burgeoning*** at a frantic pace.
10 The party split because of unmanageable ***internecine*** conflicts.

Stage 2 Match the words and expressions with their definitions or synonyms:

a) ___ [ADJECTIVE]: gullible, credulous, ingenuous
b) ___ [VERB]: go over again, sum up
c) ___ [NOUN]: the morally accepted behavior
d) ___ [ADJECTIVE]: internal
e) ___ [ADJECTIVE]: leading, favorable
f) ___ [VERB]: grow, develop
g) ___ [NOUN]: use of clever tactic or technique, ingenuity
h) ___ [ADJECTIVE]: cumbersome
i) ___ [ADJECTIVE]: timely, opportune
j) ___ [ADJECTIVE]: pretty, beautiful, attractive

EXAM PRACTICE 8
GRAMMAR

Part 1 Multiple-choice

1 At no time ___ aware of the risks I was running.

a) I was
b) was I
c) I do
d) I did

2 Polite ___ he may be, he can sometimes be stupid.

a) although
b) however
c) though
d) like

3 I hate my boss. ___ I do, he's never satisfied.

a) Whatever

b) Whichever

c) What

d) That

4 I find ___ strange to start a relationship on the internet.

a) it's

b) that

c) that''s

d) it

5 It is vital that all the students ___ the meeting.

a) attend

b) attends

c) would attend

d) will attend

6 Handing in your assignments when they're due is mandatory, ___ you might not pass.

a) likewise

b) otherwise

c) furthermore

d) in as much as

7 ___ the problem of landfills is concerned, the mayor says they're looking for a solution.

a) As to

b) As for

c) As with

d) As far as

8 "How long ___ in Europe?"

a) are you

b) did you
c) do you stay
d) have you been

9 ___ led to his eligibility for a scholarship.
a) He was dedicated to his studies
b) His dedication to the studies
c) Because he was dedicated to his studies
d) He dedicated to his studies

10 The extinction of dinosaurs is ___ caused by meteorite collisions.
a) thought it was
b) thought to have been
c) thought to has been
d) thought to had been

11 I remember ___ the door, but I just can't find my keys.
a) to close
b) that I closed
c) closing
d) close

12 I was having difficulty dealing with the customers, but everything was fine ___ the end.
a) by
b) for
c) at
d) in

13 Sometimes I wish I ___ a stubborn person.
a) wasn't
b) am not
c) wouldn't be
d) am

14 I'm so upset I wasted my time. I ___ the exercise.

a) didn't need to do

b) needn't have done

c) needn't had done

d) didn't need do

15 Hardly ever ___ people who are really appreciative.

a) I find

b) there's

c) I'm finding

d) do I find

16 Where have you been? I haven't seen you ___ Christmas!

a) for

b) at

c) since

d) on

17 When you fill out the questionnaire, try to answer as ___ questions as you can.

a) much

b) many

c) few

d) little

18 ___ your complaint, we are happy to inform you that a solution has already been found.

a) With regard to

b) As regards to

c) In regard

d) In regards to

19 ___ you have a great time during your vacation.

a) May

b) That
c) Might
d) Do

20 What beautiful glasses. Could you tell me where ___ them?
a) you've bought
b) have you bought
c) did you buy
d) you buy

Part 2 Key word transformation

Follow the same instructions as in Exam Practice 1.

1 If I were you, I'd take an umbrella. **(better)**
You ____________________________ an umbrella.

2 The teacher didn't talk about the exams until the end of the month. **(did)**
Not until the end of the month ____________________________ about the exams.

3 All the students are expected to know the rules. **(supposed)**
The rules ____________________________ by all the students.

4 Nobody will leave classroom earlier. **(is)**
Nobody ____________________________ earlier.

5 You should have left a message. **(ought)**
You ____________________________ a message.

6 My brother and I have a good relationship. **(along)**
My brother and I ____________________________ with each other.

7 "It was not my fault," she said. **(out)**
"Don't ____________________________ me," she said.

8 No sooner had I gone to bed than I heard a noise. **(only)**
I had ____________________________ I heard a noise.

9 I didn't find it hard to do the test. **(difficulty)**
I had ____________________________ the test.

10 I wasn't surprised at the result. **(came)**
The result ____________________________ to me.

ROUND OFF 8

1 Match the two halves:

a) ***resort***

b) a ***righteous***

c) a ... under ***warranty***

d) ***extol***

e) keep ***abreast*** of

f) ***atmospheric***

g) a ***withering***

h) ***gateway*** to

i) a ***household***

j) ***cogently***

1) ___ the latest information

2) ___ to violence

3) ___ product

4) ___ argue

5) ___ music

6) ___ name

7) ___ someone's virtues
8) ___ look
9) ___ success
10) ___ person

2 Now match the words in boldface in A with the following synonyms or definitions:

1) ___ upright
2) ___ door
3) ___ make use of
4) ___ disturbing
5) ___ praise
6) ___ well informed
7) ___ guarantee
8) ___ pleasant
9) ___ convincingly
10) ___ popular

3 Match the words underlined with their synonyms:

a) Don't worry about your stay. They'll do everything to help you. They're always very accommodating.

b) Knowing a foreign language nowadays is a must have asset.

c) It was unsettling for the teachers to hear about the syndicate's decision.

d) She didn't own up, but her facial expression was tantamount to a confession.

e) After working for hours without eating the workers were ravenous.

f) They accused him of involvement in some nefarious activities.

g) Even though he was very rich, he used to wear nondescript clothes.

h) Canoeing under the moonlight was an idyllic experience in that summer.

i) Tourism is now a burgeoning industry, since traveling has become more accessible.

j) Internecine fighting among the members of the party has brought a lot of problems.

1) ___ disturbing
2) ___ famished
3) ___ dull
4) ___ cooperative
5) ___ pleasant
6) ___ increasing
7) ___ resource
8) ___ internal
9) ___ shameful
10) ___ comparable

4 Match words from exercise 3 (A – J) with their antonyms (not all of them have been used):

1) ___ satisfied
2) ___ remarkable
3) ___ reassuring
4) ___ external
5) ___ shrinking
6) ___ virtuous
7) ___ disobliging

5 WORD FORMATION

NOUN	VERB	ADJECTIVE	ADVERB
		righteous	
		dazzling	
			cogently
		beguiling	
		idyllic	
	reproach		
		felicitous	
		naive	
bigotry			

Key to lessons 36 - 40

LESSON 36 – a) 9 b) 8 c) 4 d) 6 e) 10 f) 3 g) 1 h) 2 i) 5 j) 7
LESSON 37 – a) 5 b) 6 c) 2 d) 1 e) 4 f) 7 g) 9 h) 10 i) 3 j) 8
LESSON 38 – a) 6 b) 1 c) 9 d) 10 e) 5 f) 3 g) 8 h) 7 i) 2 j) 4
LESSON 39 – a) 4 b) 7 c) 1 d) 9 e) 3 f) 5 g) 10 h) 8 i) 2 j) 6
LESSON 40 – a) 1 b) 4 c) 6 d) 10 e) 3 f) 9 g) 7 h) 5 i) 2 j) 8

EXAM PRACTICE 8

PART I

1 B) The inversion is used for emphasis.
2 C) (= "Although he may be polite, he can...")
3 A) (= "It doesn't matter what I do, he's never...")
4 D) "It" is what is called a "preparatory object" here.
5 A) "Attend" here is being used in the subjunctive. "Should" is implicit after "student".
6 B) (= "... or else you might not pass.")
7 D) (= "In regard to the problem of landfills...")
8 D) "How long" + present perfect: someone is asking about the duration of something which started in past and continues into the present.
9 B) "His dedication to the studies" acts as the subject of the verb which begins the new sentence: "led to..."
10 B) (= "It is thought that the extinction of dinosaurs has been caused...") Check a grammar book for the use of the perfect passive.
11 C) "Remember" is followed by a gerund when we're talking about the past. In this use, "remember" is not followed by "that". Compare: "Remember (that) you have to finish your report." (In this case it is possible because it refers to the future.)
12 D) Note: "At the end" is used to specify precisely: "At the end of the month / the book..." etc. "In the end" is close in meaning to "finally".
13 A) "I wish" is followed by the simple past when we refer to a real condition (= "I am stubborn, but I wouldn't like to be.") Note that "weren't" would be a formal option.
14 B) "I needn't have done" means that I did it, even though it wasn't necessary. "I didn't need to do" means that it wasn't necessary and I didn't do it.
15 D) (= "I hardly ever find...") In sentences beginning with "Hardly ever", the interrogative structure is used for emphasis (inversion).
16 C) "Since" is used with the present perfect to show the duration of a period.
17 B) "Many" is used here because it is followed by a countable plural noun.

18 A) "In regard to" (that is, "considering") would also be possible.
19 A) (= "I hope you have a great time...")
20 A) Note that this is an indirect question, therefore you should not use an interrogative structure.

PART II
1 ***had better take***
2 ***did the teacher talk***
3 ***are supposed to be known***
4 ***is to leave classroom***
5 ***ought to have left***
6 ***get along well***
7 ***take it out on***
8 ***only just gone to bed when***
9 ***no difficulty (in) doing***
10 ***came as no surprise***

ROUNDING OFF 8
1 1 e 2 a 3 c 4 j 5 f 6 i 7 d 8 g 9 h 10) b
2 1 b 2) h 3) a 4) g 5) d 6) e 7) c 8) f 9) j 10) i
3 1) c 2) e 3) g 4) a 5) h 6) i 7) b 8) j 9) f 10) d
4 1) e 2) g 3) c 4) j 5) i 6) f 7) a
5 WORD FORMATION

NOUN	VERB	ADJECTIVE	ADVERB
righteousness	x	***righteous***	righteously
x	dazzle	***dazzling***	x
cogency	x	cogent	***cogently***
x	beguile	***beguiling***	beguilingly
idyll	x	***idyllic***	x
x	***reproach***	reproachful	reproachfully
felicity	x	***felicitous***	felicitously
naivety	x	***naive***	naively
bigotry	x	bigoted	x

10 MINUTES A DAY

LESSON 41

Stage 1 Read the sentences carefully and try to figure out the meaning of the word or expression in bold from the context. Then, go on to the next Stage.

1 I have no ***qualms*** about quitting school. I didn't have choice.
2 Scientists ***prognosticate*** that a cure for cancer will soon be found.
3 During the wake, the priest read a long, ***elegiac*** poem in honor of the dead.
4 If you are disobedient, you'll provoke the gods' ***wrath***.
5 All those misfortunes from the past have now sank into blissful ***oblivion***.
6 There's no point in complaining to the teacher about your grades. She's very ***opinionated***.
7 The worker was dismissed because he was accused of ***blackmail***.
8 Have all the students been fully ***apprised*** of their obligations?
9 The audience was ***aghast*** at the gratuitous violence in the movie.
10 Besides being a very competent and humble worker, he is aware of his own ***shortcomings***.

Stage 2 Match the words and expressions with their definitions or synonyms:

a) ___ [NOUN]: forgetfulness, unconcern
b) ___ [VERB]: foreshadow, predict
c) ___ [NOUN]: money extortion
d) ___ [ADJECTIVE]: startled, shocked
e) ___ [NOUN]: nagging doubts, remorse
f) ___ [NOUN]: weakness, fault, imperfection
g) ___ [NOUN]: fury, indignation
h) ___ [ADJECTIVE]: stubborn, intransigent, inflexible
i) ___ [ADJECTIVE]: mournful, sorrowful
j) ___ [VERB]: tell, inform

10 MINUTES A DAY

LESSON 42

Stage 1 Read the sentences carefully and try to figure out the meaning of the word or expression in bold from the context. Then, go on to the next Stage.

1 The campers showed ***blithe*** disregard for safety rules.
2 The article in which the regulations were published was so ***convoluted*** that hardly anyone could understand it.
3 People who work as caretakers need to show great ***forbearance*** to take care of older people.
4 The executives embarked on a ***mammoth*** undertaking when they decided to merge the two companies.
5 The problem with his novels is that the plot is so ***pedestrian*** and the characters are mediocre.
6 In this company you are expected to work hard. You shouldn't be ***remiss*** in your responsibilities.
7 When I'm driving on my way to the coast, I feel as tough I'm caught up in a ***revelry***.
8 The principal had a ***stentorian*** voice which imposed respect and admiration among students.
9 Our friendship remains ***steadfast*** as it has always been and will always be.
10 The students feel diminished in the presence of that teacher. He's so ***supercilious*** and arrogant.

Stage 2 Match the words and expressions with their definitions or synonyms:

a) ___ [NOUN]: patience, tolerance
b) ___ [ADJECTIVE]: carefree, jaunty, nonchalant
c) ___ [ADJECTIVE]: lacking in style, unimaginative
d) ___ [ADJECTIVE]: disdainful, snobbish, superior
e) ___ [ADJECTIVE]: very loud
f) ___ [ADJECTIVE]: sloppy, negligent
g) ___ [ADJECTIVE]: gigantic (figuratively: very big)
h) ___ [ADJECTIVE]: intricate, entangled (in a way that is complicated)
i) ___ [ADJECTIVE]: unwavering, loyal
j) ___ [NOUN]: gaiety, spree, happiness

10 MINUTES A DAY

LESSON 43

Stage 1 Read the sentences carefully and try to figure out the meaning of the word or expression in bold from the context. Then, go on to the next Stage.

1 I don't like taking my children to restaurants because they're so ***finicky*** about eating.
2 The students live on an ***allowance*** offered by the university to support them.
3 Indians' customs have been completely ***misconstrued*** in the soap opera.
4 The movie was a success, but it has been criticized for its many ***lewd*** scenes.
5 The disease is still in an ***incipient*** phase now. We'll have to wait until we can understand it better.
6 You just can't ***gainsay*** these plain truths. Why don't you accept this fact?
7 Students may become ***diffident*** if they feel inadequate in classroom.
8 I had the ***uncanny*** sensation that I was being followed by a stalker.
9 Chaos and political unrest ***ensued*** after the death of the political leader.
10 Her recipe for a long life is eating with ***frugality*** and avoiding alcohol.

Stage 2 Match the words and expressions with their definitions or synonyms:

a) ___ [VERB]: misinterpret, distort
b) ___ [ADJECTIVE]: impeding, inchoate, beginning
c) ___ [ADJECTIVE]: creepy, eerie, strange
d) ___ [ADJECTIVE]: picky, fussy, over particular
e) ___ [VERB]: deny
f) ___ [NOUN]: moderation, husbandry, thrift
g) ___ [NOUN]: grant, financial aid
h) ___ [ADJECTIVE]: bashful, shy, insecure
i) ___ [ADJECTIVE]: lecherous, vulgar, indecent
j) ___ [VERB]: follow as a result of something

10 MINUTES A DAY

LESSON 44

Stage 1 Read the sentences carefully and try to figure out the meaning of the word or expression in bold from the context. Then, go on to the next Stage.

1 These antibiotics help to ***ward off*** the slightest possibility of infection.
2 You are such a ***gullible*** person to fall for his feeble excuses.
3 The students didn't take the teachers' advice seriously and failed ***dismally*** in the exam.
4 The wealthy family lived in a ***stately*** mansion in the city suburbs.
5 Some may think it is offensive to refer to people as mentally ***handicapped***.
6 Our boss is very proud of his reputation and likes us to see him as ***upright*** and fair.
7 We have come to an impasse, so we should make an effort to reach a ***compromise***.
8 We encourage our workers to ***reconcile*** when they fight because of disagreement.
9 The other workers looked up to him because he was an experienced ***veteran***.
10 The journalist is known for his ***incisive*** analysis of the government's policies.

Stage 2 Match the words and expressions with their definitions or synonyms:

a) ___ [NOUN]: give and take, settlement, agreement
b) ___ [ADJECTIVE]: righteous, virtuous
c) ___ [ADJECTIVE]: sharp, perspicacious, intelligent
d) ___ [ADJECTIVE]: restrained, disabled
e) ___ [VERB]: defend, guard, keep away
f) ___ [ADVERB]: terribly
g) ___ [ADJECTIVE]: majestic, sumptuous
h) ___ [VERB]: make peace, appease, settle
i) ___ [NOUN]: a seasoned, experienced person
j) ___ [ADJECTIVE]: credulous, ingenuous

10 MINUTES A DAY

LESSON 45

Stage 1 Read the sentences carefully and try to figure out the meaning of the word or expression in bold from the context. Then, go on to the next Stage.

1 I'm in a bit of a ***predicament*** because I didn't save any money.
2 The student grew ***despondent*** about having failed his exams dismally.
3 The student's lamentable depression seriously ***hindered*** his progress at school.
4 Those poor people from the interior were living in ***abysmal***, blithe ignorance.
5 In those distant and depressing places people lived their ***barren*** lives without any perspectives.
6 My father was so ***fastidious*** about everything he did. I just couldn't tolerate it.
7 I sometimes like to ***indulge*** myself in a shopping spree to relieve tension!
8 With the high temperature, I was feeling miserable and ***lethargic***.
9 He wrote a ***concise*** article and published it in a prestigious magazine.
10 Having a good reputation is of ***inestimable*** value to a scientist.

Stage 2 Match the words and expressions with their definitions or synonyms:

a) ___ [NOUN]: quandary, difficulty
b) ___ [ADJECTIVE]: choosy, over particular, meticulous
c) ___ [ADJECTIVE]: very bad, terrible
d) ___ [ADJECTIVE]: restrained, disabled
e) ___ [VERB]: slow down, hamper, impede
f) ___ [ADJECTIVE]: short, brief
g) ___ [ADJECTIVE]: dejected, gloomy, sad
h) ___ [VERB]: allow yourself to have too much of something
i) ___ [ADJECTIVE]: lazy, without any energy
j) ___ [ADJECTIVE]: incalculable

EXAM PRACTICE 9
GRAMMAR

Part 1 Multiple-choice

1 ___ all the food and drinking, it's no wonder your stomach is upset now.
a) Having
b) Because
c) What with
d) For

2 ___ him complaining about his grade, you'd think he'd performed poorly in the exam.
a) Hearing
b) Heard
c) To hear
d) Had heard

3 I hushed to get to the airport earlier, only ___ that I'd stupidly left my passport back at home.

a) to find out
b) finding out
c) I found out
d) just found out

4 ___ to take my pill, I started to fill sick.

a) I didn't remember
b) Not having remembered
c) Not remembered
d) Because I remembered

5 Unless ___ indicated, do not write in the spaces below here.

a) being
b) otherwise
c) its
d) if

6 There are lots of books. Choose ___ one you want.

a) whichever
b) whoever
c) whatsoever
d) whenever

7 There was some disagreement ___ the man could adopt the child or not.

a) about
b) about if
c) as to whether
d) because

8 Don't feel embarrassed. We'll be grateful for ___ help you can give.

a) whichever
b) whatever

c) anything
d) what

9 This book was written to meet the needs of Spanish and Portuguese learners ___.
a) like
b) alike
c) both
d) likewise

10 It's been ___since you last paid me a visit.
a) awhile
b) a while
c) time
d) far

11 The flight was canceled due ___.
a) to the bad weather
b) it was a bad weather
c) that the weather was bad
d) the bad weather

12 Tourism is more expensive now ___, as a result, people have decided not to travel.
a) but
b) however
c) notwithstanding
d) and

13 We may be able to put you up for a week or two ___ you try to find a job.
a) meanwhile
b) while
c) whereas
d) otherwise

14 First I made him a call, sent him an email and ___ succeeded in meeting him personally.

a) lastly

b) for last

c) at last

d) at the end

15 ___ made you ask me that stupid question?

a) Whenever

b) That

c) Whatever

d) Which

16 More people ___ nowadays than ever before.

a) have been caught stealing

b) has been caught stealing

c) have been caught stolen

d) have caught stolen

17 After ___ his exercise, he decided to take some rest.

a) finished

b) he has finished

c) finishing

d) finishes

18 He was told ___ late.

a) to not stay up

b) not stay up

c) not to stay up

d) don't stay up

19 The teacher suggested ___ private classes.

a) us to have

b) that we have

c) us have
d) we should had

20 "What's the matter with John?"
"He's worried ___ the exam."
a) for his brother failed
b) about his brother's failing
c) his brother failed
d) because his brother failing

Part 2 Key word transformation

Follow the same instructions as in Exam Practice 1.

1 He's the most intelligent person I've ever met. **(such)**
I've never ___________________________ person in all my life.

2 I couldn't hear him because the TV was too loud. **(that)**
The TV ___________________________ couldn't hear him.

3 You'll have to study hard to follow the rest of the class. **(catch)**
You'll have to study hard ________________________ the rest of the class.

4 I don't like her, but she is a great teacher. **(despite)**
___________________________ like her, she is a great teacher.

5 He studied hard because he wanted a good grade. **(order)**
He studied hard ___________________________ a good grade.

6 I would love to come, but I won't be able. **(much)**
___________________________, I won't be able.

7 She worked hard to make a good impression at work. **(as)**
She worked hard ___________________________ at work.

8 The room was noisy, but I could concentrate on the exam. **(though)**
____________________________, I could concentrate on the exam.

9 I wish you would learn to make your own bed. **(high)**
It's ____________________________ how to make your own bed.

10 If only I had travelled more when I was younger. **(taken)**
I ____________________________ to travel more when I was younger.

ROUND OFF 9

1 Match the columns to find the synonyms of the words underlined:

1) It is necessary to apprise all the workers of their responsibilities.
2) My mother was aghast at the obscene language in the song lyrics.
3) The children played cheerfully with blithe disregard for safety.
4) If you want recognition, you cannot be remiss in your career.
5) Our marriage has been steadfast. I was happy to find a good husband.
6) Our boss was supercilious. He looked down on everybody at the company.
7) This creepy place gives me an uncanny sensation that there's somebody around.
8) Children become diffident if they're downtrodden in classroom.
9) The candidates failed dismally in the math test. They didn't expect it to be so difficult.
10) Don't go on with this quarrel. Why can't you reconcile?

a) ___ unchanging
b) ___ badly
c) ___ inform
d) ___ appease

e) ___ carefree
f) ___ mysterious
g) ___ horrified
h) ___ superior
i) ___ negligent
j) ___ insecure

2 Fill in the spaces with one of these words:

qualms	*finicky*
opinionated	*misconstrued*
shortcomings	*compromise*
pedestrian	*predicament*
stentorian	*despondent*

a) The student grew increasingly ___ when he realized he was certain to fail.
b) I have no ___ about dismissing those careless workers. They deserve it.
c) Even though he had some ___ as a teacher, he was a lovely person.
d) You're in a real ___ when you don't have any money to rely on.
e) Strikers and employers weren't able to ___ on a deal.
f) The teacher had a ___ voice that helped him get students' attention.
g) Even tough he's very young, he's pretty ___. He won't change his mind sometimes.
h) Her poem didn't win the contest because it was considered pretty ___.
i) My children are ___ eaters. I wish they would eat everything.
j) The politician said his declarations were ___ on purpose by the press.

3 Match the answers from A – J above with one of these synonyms:
1) ___ uneasiness
2) ___ hardship
3) ___ resounding
4) ___ dejected
5) ___ stubborn

6) _ _ _ banal
7) _ _ _ weakness
8) _ _ _ choosy
9) _ _ _ misinterpret
10) _ _ _ concede

4 WORD FORMATION

NOUN	VERB	ADJECTIVE	ADVERB
	prognosticate		
		elegiac	
		blithe	
		lewd	
		diffident	
frugality			
compromise			
	reconcile		
		despondent	

Key to lessons 41 – 45

LESSON 41 – a) 5 b) 2 c) 7 d) 9 e) 1 f) 10 g) 4 h) 6 i) 3 j) 8
LESSON 42 – a) 3 b) 1 c) 5 d) 10 e) 8 f) 6 g) 4 h) 2 i) 9 j) 7
LESSON 43 – a) 3 b) 5 c) 8 d) 1 e) 6 f) 10 g) 2 h) 7 i) 4 j) 9
LESSON 44 – a) 7 b) 6 c) 10 d) 5 e) 1 f) 3 g) 4 h) 8 i) 9 j) 2
LESSON 45 – a) 1 b) 6 c) 4 d) 5 e) 3 f) 9 g) 2 h) 7 i) 8 j) 10

EXAM PRACTICE 9

PART I

1 C) "What with", followed by a "noun phrase", is used to introduce a reason. It is close in meaning to: "Because you ate and drank so much…"
2 C) (= "... if you heard him complaining...")
3 A) "… only to find out" is a fixed grammar pattern.
4 B) "Not having remembered" expresses the cause (check a grammar book for reduced adverbial clauses.)
5 B) (= "Unless there's indication to the contrary, do not write...")
6 A) (whichever one = any of them)
7 C) (= "regarding…")
8 B) (whatever help = any help)
9 B) (= "... was written to meet the needs of both Spanish and Portuguese learners.")
10 B) (a while = some time)
11 A) (= "... because of the bad weather.")
12 D) "And" is used here to introduce both addition and consequence.
13 B) (= "... for a week or two during the time in which you try to find a job.")
14 A) We use "lastly" to mention the last item of a sequence.
15 C) We use "whatever", instead of "what", to express surprise in a more emphatic way (mainly spoken).
16 A) (= "The police have been catching more people stealing nowadays than ever before.") Pay attention to the structure transformation into the passive voice.
17 C) "After" is a preposition. Therefore, we should use the gerund after it. However, it would also be possible: "After he finished his exercise…"
18 C) Someone told him: "Don't stay up late." In reported speech, "don't" becomes "not to" + infinitive.
19 B) In this meaning, "suggest" has to be followed by "that" + subject pronoun ("suggest that we"), and never by an "object pronoun" (suggest us to). Alternatively, "that" can be omitted: "The teacher suggested we have…"

20 B) "Worried" takes the preposition "about", which in this structure is followed by a noun. In this case, "failing" (gerund) exerts the role of a noun.

PART II

1 ***met such an intelligent***
2 ***was so loud that***
3 ***to catch up with***
4 ***Despite the fact that I don't***
5 ***in order to get***
6 ***Much as I would love to come***
7 ***so as to make a good impression***
8 ***Noisy though the room was***
9 ***high time you learned***
10 ***wish I had taken the chance***

ROUNDING OFF 9

1 a) 5 b) 9 c) 1 d) 10 e) 3 f) 7 g) 2 h) 6 i) 4 j) 8
2 a) despondent
b) qualms
c) shortcomings
d) predicament
e) compromise
f) stentorian
g) opinionated
h) pedestrian
i) finicky
j) misconstrued
3 1) b 2) d 3) f 4) a 5) g 6) h 7) c 8) i 9) j 10) e
4 WORD FORMATION

NOUN	VERB	ADJECTIVE	ADVERB
prognostication	***prognosticate***	x	x
elegy (eulogy)	x	***elegiac***	x
x	x	***blithe***	blithely
lewdness	x	***lewd***	x
diffidence	x	***diffident***	diffidently
frugality	x	frugal	frugally
compromise	compromise	compromising	x
reconciliation	***reconcile***	reconciling	x
despondency	x	***despondent***	despondently

10 MINUTES A DAY

LESSON 46

Stage 1 Read the sentences carefully and try to figure out the meaning of the word or expression in bold from the context. Then, go on to the next Stage.

1 The school authorities are working hard to ***avert*** a crisis among students.
2 My mother is very supportive of my career plans, while my father is always making ***disparaging*** remarks about them.
3 Many scientists have not become famous exactly because of their intelligence, but for their ***wacky*** ideas.
4 The guy who shot his ex-girlfriend had been ***harboring*** a grudge against her for a long time.
5 He was detested by everyone because he was an unkind, ***vicious*** person.
6 He hasn't made any real effort to overcome his wife's death. On the contrary, he's been ***wallowing*** in depression ever since she died.
7 The student tried to leave the classroom ***surreptitiously***, but his plan fell through.
8 Since his boss told him he would not be promoted, his enthusiasm has been ***withering*** visibly.
9 The judge has ***summoned*** us to appear in court to give our testimony.
10 Her conduct is most ***reprehensible***. Everyone is appalled at her bad behavior.

Stage 2 Match the words and expressions with their definitions or synonyms:

a) ___ [ADVERB]: stealthily, furtively
b) ___ [ADJECTIVE]: deserving condemnation
c) ___ [ADJECTIVE]: offbeat, eccentric
d) ___ [ADJECTIVE]: brutal, cruel
e) ___ [ADJECTIVE]: belittling, derisive, denigrating
f) ___ [VERB]: shelter, keep a thought in your mind for too long (figuratively)
g) ___ [VERB]: roll about (in a figurative sense: indulge in, revel)
h) ___ [VERB]: turn away, prevent
i) ___ [VERB]: dry up (in a figurative sense: weaken, decline, wane)
j) ___ [VERB]: order

10 MINUTES A DAY

LESSON 47

Stage 1 Read the sentences carefully and try to figure out the meaning of the word or expression in bold from the context. Then, go on to the next Stage.

1 Where I work I am ***answerable*** for anything that goes wrong.
2 After a month's work, the inexperienced nurse was left feeling ***frazzled***.
3 All those ***convoluted*** explanations and schemes didn't make any sense to me.
4 We're working at a ***frantic*** pace to avert a financial crisis at the company.
5 He was a remarkably ***adroit*** person whose work was admired by everyone.
6 Saying that the United States is a place of opportunities has become a ***commonplace***.
7 Everyone thought she was very strange, ***presumably*** because she had survived a tragic accident.
8 In order to ***redress*** the balance, let's give students another opportunity for them to hand in their belated assignments.
9 The hypothesis put forward by the researchers was much too ***tenuous*** to get any serious attention.
10 It was extremely ***reassuring*** to hear that she had already overcome her illness.

Stage 2 Match the words and expressions with their definitions or synonyms:

a) ___ [ADJECTIVE]: intricate, complicated
b) ___ [VERB]: remedy, set right, make fair
c) ___ [ADJECTIVE]: restoring confidence
d) ___ [ADJECTIVE]: responsible, accountable, liable
e) ___ [ADJECTIVE]: flimsy, weak
f) ___ [ADJECTIVE]: mentally exhausted
g) ___ [ADJECTIVE]: skillful
h) ___ [VERB]: trite, ordinary, customary
i) ___ [ADVERB]: very likely
j) ___ [ADJECTIVE]: frenzied, agitated, frenetic

10 MINUTES A DAY

LESSON 48

Stage 1 Read the sentences carefully and try to figure out the meaning of the word or expression in bold from the context. Then, go on to the next Stage.

1 Completing my doctorate degree now is my ***overriding*** concern.
2 The teacher is making a lot of effort to get his ***tenure***, after all security is important.
3 She was a nice, ***gregarious*** person. She loved her friends' company.
4 The whole city was terribly ***distraught*** at the news of the young teenagers' death.
5 You couldn't miss him because of his ***conspicuous*** mullet hairstyle.
6 The protesters were accused of ***inciting*** violence and vandalism.
7 This company has become a ***juggernaut*** in its field.
8 Robert always ***eschews*** any questions about his private life.
9 I was fed up with her ***facetious*** comments about my job.
10 The teacher had an ***ineffable*** ability to captivate students' attention.

Stage 2 Match the words and expressions with their definitions or synonyms:

a) ___ **[NOUN]**: the right to keep a job until someone retires
b) ___ **[VERB]**: coax, motivate, instigate
c) ___ **[ADJECTIVE]**: sociable, enjoying other people's company
d) ___ **[VERB]**: shun, shy away, avoid
e) ___ **[ADJECTIVE]**: witty, jocular, sarcastic
f) ___ **[ADJECTIVE]**: main, paramount, predominant
g) ___ **[ADJECTIVE]**: noticeable, evident
h) ___ **[NOUN]**: a large truck (figuratively: big and powerful, in a negative sense.)
i) ___ **[ADJECTIVE]**: too great to be described, something that cannot be easily expressed
j) ___ **[ADJECTIVE]**: upset, distressed, worried

10 MINUTES A DAY

LESSON 49

Stage 1 Read the sentences carefully and try to figure out the meaning of the word or expression in bold from the context. Then, go on to the next Stage.

1 The defendant ***avowed*** that he was unaware of what was going on.
2 Fearing a ***reprisal***, the political party didn't attack its opponents.
3 The teacher couldn't stand the student's ***sardonic*** sense of humor.
4 The writer wanted to be part of the notorious ***clique*** of bohemians.
5 The student tried to put some finishing touches to ***embellish*** his composition.
6 The dancer had an uncanny ***flair*** for dancing the tango.
7 The student ***importuned*** the teacher for another chance to take the test.
8 He's an unscrupulous, ***opportunistic*** man who will do whatever he can to defeat his opponents.
9 After he retired from a challenging career, he chose a more ***prosaic*** life in the countryside.
10 Tourists are ***wary*** of traveling to that region after the natural disasters which struck it.

Stage 2 Match the words and expressions with their definitions or synonyms:

a) ___ [NOUN]: vengeance, retaliation
b) ___ [VERB]: enhance, beautify, adorn
c) ___ [NOUN]: mastery, ability, aptitude
d) ___ [VERB]: acknowledge, aver, declare openly
e) ___ [ADJECTIVE]: clever, astute, strategic
f) ___ [ADJECTIVE]: worried, prudent, cautious
g) ___ [ADJECTIVE]: acerbic, caustic, sarcastic
h) ___ [NOUN]: a small, exclusive group of friends
i) ___ [ADJECTIVE]: pedestrian, ordinary, simple
j) ___ [VERB]: pester, harass, badger, beg insistently

10 MINUTES A DAY

LESSON

50

Stage 1 Read the sentences carefully and try to figure out the meaning of the word or expression in bold from the context. Then, go on to the next Stage.

1. The war veteran became a ***recluse***. He didn't have any friends.
2. The students always ***procrastinate*** when it comes to handing in their homework.
3. He was ***crestfallen*** after having lost the game.
4. Knowing all the words of a language is a ***chimerical*** target.
5. Drinking alcohol ***impairs*** your capacity to operate machines.
6. The promotion of workers to higher positions is ***contingent*** on their record.
7. They gave a highly ***implausible*** explanation for the team's failure.
8. She ***inadvertently*** deleted all the files in the archive. It wasn't on purpose.
9. After ***protracted*** negotiations at long last the strikers have decided to go back to work.
10. He was once a rich man, but he had such a ***prodigal*** lifestyle that he is now ruined.

Stage 2 Match the words and expressions with their definitions or synonyms:

a) ___ **[ADVERB]**: heedlessly, negligently
b) ___ **[VERB]**: harm, hinder, debilitate
c) ___ **[ADJECTIVE]**: lasting for longer than it is desired
d) ___ **[VERB]**: put off doing something indefinitely
e) ___ **[ADJECTIVE]**: delusive, utopian, absurd
f) ___ **[ADJECTIVE]**: dependent on, conditional
g) ___ **[ADJECTIVE]**: dejected, dispirited, sad
h) ___ **[ADJECTIVE]**: squandering, dissipated, extravagant
i) ___ **[NOUN]**: withdrawn, hermit, loner
j) ___ **[ADJECTIVE]**: inconceivable, unreasonable

EXAM PRACTICE 10
GRAMMAR

Part 1 Multiple-choice

1 "When can we leave classroom?"
"When the class ___."
a) will finish
b) has been finished
c) finished
d) finishes

2 I am not ___ early.
a) accustomed to getting up
b) used to get up
c) used getting up
d) accustomed to get up

3 "Was the examination difficult?"
"I've never taken ___ before."

a) so difficult a test
b) such difficult test
c) so difficult test
d) such a test difficult

4 I tried and tried, but the car ___.

a) does not start
b) should not start
c) will not start
d) might not start

5 Only by studying hard ___ good grades.

a) you will get
b) will you get
c) you get
d) you're getting

6 Not only ___ write songs, but also poems.

a) he
b) does he
c) he does
d) him

7 I didn't do my exercise, and ___ my brother.

a) neither did
b) also didn't
c) didn't too
d) didn't either

8 ___, would you vote for him?

a) If Ron runs for mayor
b) If Ron run for mayor

c) Were Ron to run for mayor
d) If Ron would run for mayor

9 You can leave earlier, ___ you finish all your exercises.
a) provided that
b) providing
c) unless
d) if only

10 ___ be so kind as to open the window?
a) Would you
b) You would
c) Could you
d) May you be

11 I was late, ___.
a) like was my brother
b) like my brother was
c) as was my brother
d) as my brother was

12 I ate too much at lunch, ___.
a) as my father did
b) as did my father
c) as was my father
d) like my father did

13 I didn't know what to say, and ___ my friends.
a) nor did
b) as did
c) neither
d) either

14 ___ as I might, I didn't get a good grade.

a) Tried
b) Trying
c) I tried
d) Try

15 The harder you exercise, ___ you get.

a) fitter
b) the fitter
c) more fit
d) fittest

16 I had the painter ___ my house last weekend.

a) painting
b) paint
c) painted
d) paints

17 I missed the train. By the time I arrived at the station, it ___.

a) already had left
b) had already left
c) hadn't left
d) was about to leave

18 ___ to another country, he didn't have a passport.

a) He never traveled
b) He had never traveled
c) Never had he traveled
d) Never having traveled

19 I wasn't counting ___ so many guests at the party.

a) on there being
b) with having
c) for being
d) on it having

20 Paul wanted to stay at home instead of ___ around with my friends.

a) he hang

b) hanging

c) he hanging

d) him hanging

Part 2 Key word transformation

Follow the same instructions as in Exam Practice 1.

1 I think it would be better if you found the solution for yourself. **(prefer)**
I would ____________________________ for yourself.

2 You look tired. You probably worked hard all day. **(must)**
You ____________________________ hard all day.

3 She would prefer to be allowed the chance to rehearse it more. **(were)**
She thinks it would be better ____________________________ to rehearse it more.

4 I regret not studying as hard as I could when I was at college. **(only)**
If ____________________________ I could when I was at college.

5 I suggest that you follow the rules without complaining. **(better)**
You would ____________________________ without complaining.

6 There was no need to fill out the questionnaire. **(have)**
You ____________________________ the questionnaire.

7 The teacher told the students the strike would almost certainly happen. **(likelihood)**
The teacher told the students ____________________________ happen.

8 If the examiners catch anyone cheating, the candidate is disqualified. **(caught)**

If ___________________________, the candidate is disqualified.

9 Everyone thinks he was sentenced unfairly. **(thought)**

He is ___________________________ unfairly.

10 She's only a teenager, but she is extremely intelligent. **(even)**

___________________________ a teenager, she is extremely intelligent.

ROUND OFF 10

1 Match the columns to find a synonym for the word in boldface:

a) The sanitary authorities are making efforts to ***prevent*** a scandal.

b) Scientists' ***weird*** ideas sometimes prove to be actually interesting and revolutionary.

c) You're not really sick. Why don't you stop ***indulging*** yourself in this depression?

d) The explanations were too ***intricate*** for my taste. Why don't they speak in a simpler vocabulary?

e) Saying that Americans are not good language learners has become so ***trite***.

f) What is your ***main*** concern now that you have finished college?

g) He's a ***sociable*** student. He has a lot of friends and they're always together.

h) Everyone was ***sad*** about the news of the terrible accident.

i) I just can't put up with this guy's ***caustic*** sense of humor.

j) The explanation we were given was so ***unreasonable*** we couldn't accept it.

1) ___ avert

2) ___ commonplace

3) ___ convoluted

4) ___ distraught
5) ___ gregarious
6) ___ implausible
7) ___ overriding
8) ___ sardonic
9) ___ wacky
10) ___ wallow

2 Match the two halves:

a) to make ... comments about a person's appearance
b) to give a ... smile
c) to be ... because of a flamboyant dress style
d) to be ... of statistic information
e) to make a(n) ... mistake
f) a ... battle to reach a consensus
g) to show a ... conduct
h) to deliver a ... attack on something
i) to work at a ... pace
j) to ... a question to avoid embarrassment

1) ___ frantic
2) ___ wary
3) ___ reassuring
4) ___ inadvertent
5) ___ reprehensible
6) ___ disparaging
7) ___ withering
8) ___ eschew
9) ___ protracted
10) ___ conspicuous

3 Match words 1 – 10 from exercise 2 with one of these synonyms:

a) ___ comforting
b) ___ pejorative

c) ___ frenzied
d) ___ blameworthy
e) ___ wilting
f) ___ suspicious
g) ___ evade
h) ___ noticeable
i) ___ prolonged
j) ___ unintentional

4 WORD FORMATION

NOUN	VERB	ADJECTIVE	ADVERB
		vicious	
		adroit	
		wary	
		conspicuous	
	incite		
	embellish		
			surreptitiously
		reassuring	

Key to lessons 46-50

LESSON 46 – a) 7 b) 10 c) 3 d) 5 e) 2 f) 4 g) 6 h) 1 i) 8 j) 9
LESSON 47 – a) 3 b) 8 c) 10 d) 1 e) 9 f) 2 g) 5 h) 6 i) 7 j) 4
LESSON 48 – a) 2 b) 6 c) 3 d) 8 e) 9 f) 1 g) 5 h) 7 i) 10 j) 4
LESSON 49 – a) 2 b) 5 c) 6 d) 1 e) 8 f) 10 g) h) 4 i) 9 j) 7
LESSON 50 – a) 8 b) 5 c) 9 d) 2 e) 4 f) 6 g) 3 h) 10 i) 1 j) 7

EXAM PRACTICE 10

PART I

1 D) We generally use the present simple in adverbial clauses introduced by "when".
2 A) In the expressions "be used / accustomed to", "to" is a preposition; therefore, you should use the verb in the gerund.
3 A) This is a formal alternative to "I've never taken a test so difficult."
4 C) "Will" here is used idiomatically. Check a grammar book for the idiomatic use of auxiliaries.
5 B) After certain expressions, like "only by", we should use inversion (other expressions include: on no account, at no time, not until, only now etc.)
6 B) Same justification as in 5.
7 A) (= "... and my brother didn't do it either...") In the pattern, inversion is required.
8 C) (= "If Ron ran for mayor, would you...") Review conditionals about the inversion structure in the alternative.
9 A) (= if, on condition that)
10 A) Fixed expression. No other auxiliary can be used here.
11 C) ("As was my brother" = "and so was my brother") Pay attention to the inverted word order.
12 B) (= "My father ate too much, too"). Same notes as in the preceding question.
13 A (= "neither did my friends"). Same notes as above.
14 D) (= "No matter how hard I tried, ...") Note that this is a fixed expression.
15 B) Comparatives using "the ... the ..." require a parallel structure. Therefore, after the first article we have "harder", then we should have "fitter" after the second article.
16 B (= "I arranged it for the painter to paint my house..."). Check a grammar book for the use of causative verbs.
17 We use the past perfect in a sequence of two past events to show which one happened first.
18 D) (= "Because he had never traveled...") Check a grammar book for reduced clauses.

19 A) This is the use of "there" as a preparatory subject. Check a grammar book for this use.

20 B) "Instead of" ends with a preposition; and, as the subject of the second sentence is the same as the first one (Paul), it is not necessary to repeat the subject after "instead of". Therefore, we should use "instead of + ing".

PART II

1 ***prefer it if you found the solution***
2 ***must have worked***
3 ***if she were allowed***
4 ***only I had studied as hard as***
5 ***be better off following the rules***
6 ***needn't have filled out***
7 ***there was a likelihood that the strike would***
8 ***anyone is caught cheating***
9 ***thought to have been sentenced***
10 ***Even though she's only***

ROUNDING OFF 10

1 1) a 2) e 3) d 4) h 5) g 6) j 7) f 8) i 9) b 10) c
2 1) i 2) d 3) b 4) e 5) g 6) a 7) h 8) j 9) f 10) c
3 a) 3 b) 6 c) 1 d) 5 e) 7 f) 2 g) 8 h) 10 i) 9 j) 4
4 WORD FORMATION

NOUN	VERB	ADJECTIVE	ADVERB
vice	x	***vicious***	viciously
adroitness	x	***adroit***	adroitly
wariness	x	***wary***	warily
conspicuousness	x	***conspicuous***	conspicuously
incitement	***incite***	x	x
embellishment	***embellish***	x	x
x	x	surreptitious	***surreptitiously***
reassurance	reassure	***reassuring***	reassuringly

VOCABULARY BOOSTER – FINAL REVIEW

Sharpen your skills by taking the tests below.

1 This ___ of the song by this orchestra is wonderful.

a) depiction
b) rendition
c) portrayal
d) portrait

---

2 Excessive exploitation has caused the ___ of natural resources.

a) exemption
b) depletion
c) completion
d) termination

---

3 "Beauty is in the eye of the ___," an old proverb teaches us.

a) onlooker
b) watcher
c) observer
d) beholder

---

4 The criminal was released on ___ pending an appeal.

a) bail
b) charge
c) tax
d) fee

---

5 Ignore her insults. Don't take the ___.

a) hook
b) worm
c) line
d) bait

6 The scientist was ___ for his book.

a) acclaimed

b) effluent

c) proclaimed

d) imminent

---

7 Your profile is still ___ approval.

a) mending

b) looming

c) pending

d) perusing

---

8 He had no money, but he was able to study abroad ___ to a scholarship.

a) owed

b) thanks

c) thanking

d) given

---

9 No one was able to ___ the truth about those accusations.

a) assure

b) ensure

c) ascertain

d) acclaim

---

10 I'm so bored. I'm always at ___ ends when I'm on vacation.

a) loose

b) lost

c) dead

d) no

---

11 Some readers have a short attention ___.

a) top

b) timing

c) span

d) time

12 She had no siblings. She was a(n) ___ child.

a) alone

b) aloof

c) lonely

d) only

---

13 The Oscar trophy is a ___ prize for many actors and actresses.

a) covetous

b) coveted

c) covert

d) cover

---

14 The teacher was an unfeeling man, his heart ___ of any compassion.

a) rid

b) lacking

c) free

d) devoid

---

15 High interest taxes may act as a ___ to buying cars this year.

a) disincentive

b) discourage

c) prevention

d) disillusion

---

16 It is necessary to ___ the notion that all teenagers are stupid.

a) expel

b) rebel

c) discharge

d) dispel

---

17 His violent, ___ behavior may be attributed to excessive alcohol consumption.

a) disruptive

b) abrupt

c) elusive
d) skeptical

---

18 The workers reacted to the good news with ___.
a) despondency
b) dejection
c) sadness
d) elation

---

19 Marketing often ___ us to buy unnecessary goods.
a) discourages
b) leaves
c) tricks
d) entices

---

20 Poor students are ___ paying these taxes.
a) exempt from
b) absent from
c) free to
d) dispensed of

---

21 The student was ___ from school because of his behavior.
a) expurgated
b) expelled
c) repelled
d) extolled

---

22 Young people should learn to ___ for themselves as early as possible.
a) fend
b) tend
c) bend
d) look

---

23 It ___ on my nerves when people gossip about me behind my back.
a) gets

b) goes
c) lets
d) sets

---

24 I didn't like the teacher's ___ tone. He thinks we're stupid and ignorant.
a) patronizing
b) reassuring
c) exaggerated
d) aggravating

---

25 This is a book for the ___ reader.
a) instructive
b) opinionated
c) fundamental
d) discerning

---

26 At first, the new student kept herself ___ from the rest of the classmates.
a) absent
b) aloof
c) aloft
d) absconded

---

27 I'm worn out. My routine has been ___ these days.
a) uneventful
b) spiteful
c) hectic
d) placid

---

28 My package deal to Europe fell ___ of my expectations.
a) out
b) short
c) off
d) away

29 As a loner, Paul was always ___ people.

a) infringing

b) alluring

c) pestering

d) alienating

---

30 The theory has ___ with skepticism among the scientists.

a) met

b) fallen

c) come

d) run

---

31 The man hasn't ___ his wife's passing away.

a) come out

b) done away with

c) gotten over

d) gotten away

---

32 The students made ___, enthusiastic compliments about their respectable teacher's work.

a) undeserved

b) unreserved

c) covert

d) unwarranted

---

33 Concentrate on what you're doing and don't get carried ___.

a) out

b) over

c) away

d) down

---

34 The new law ___ for a lot of criticism.

a) came in

b) fell with

c) came down
d) fell through

---

35 Calm down, will you? There is no need to fly off the ___.
a) handle
b) hand
c) head
d) belt

---

36 I'd never heard such a ___ excuse in all my life.
a) flimsy
b) loose
c) feeble
d) mild

---

37 I didn't go to work because I was feeling a little under the ___.
a) weather
b) temperature
c) sun
d) clouds

---

38 Birds of a ___ flock together.
a) group
b) family
c) wing
d) feather

---

39 You shouldn't ___ out on this opportunity.
a) be
b) go
c) miss
d) lose

---

40 He is not a dependable person and will always turn his ___ on you.
a) back

b) head
c) chest
d) hands

---

41 The number of civilian ___ in war is absurd.
a) offspring
b) offenders
c) fatalities
d) casualties

---

42 You shouldn't have paid so much for this. I think you were ___.
a) cut down on
b) ripped off
c) rolled over
d) run down

---

43 The economic crisis was ___ by the shortage of food supply.
a) brought about
b) come about
c) carried out
d) gone through

---

44 I can't ___ your discourteous behavior any more.
a) come up with
b) get by on
c) put up with
d) come by

---

45 Bees are very ___ insects.
a) gregarious
b) infamous
c) exquisite
d) obnoxious

46 Children are supposed to be ___ to their teachers.

a) detrimental

b) deleterious

c) notorious

d) deferential

---

47 I studied hard for months on end and ___ succeeded in passing.

a) lastly

b) occasionally

c) eventually

d) momentarily

---

48 The woman struggled against ___ conditions to survive.

a) adverse

b) contrary

c) elusive

d) averse

---

49 The girl ___ her gaze to avoid being bothered by the boys.

a) closes

b) averts

c) covers

d) denies

---

50 The examination date has been ___ until next week.

a) called off

b) canceled

c) moved

d) put off

---

51 I'm having a hard time trying to make ends ___.

a) meet

b) add

c) match

d) up

52 His poor performance in the exam is ___ with his behavior in class.

a) aligned

b) accountable

c) consistent

d) attributable

---

53 He was dreaming of fighting in the war because of his ___ nature.

a) belligerent

b) indulgent

c) voluble

d) uncomprehending

---

54 I was going through a hard time. I was ___.

a) safe and sound

b) tickled pink

c) up and about

d) down and out

---

55 The internet is a valuable ___ in today's educational resources.

a) contrivance

b) asset

c) fount

d) appliance

---

56 Do you think it is ___ to carry out this project?

a) feasible

b) forbidding

c) liable

d) conspicuous

---

57 After the accident, she is now ___ in hospital.

a) retiring

b) withdrawn

c) convalescing

d) retrieving

58 I cannot ___ of being sent to prison.

a) complain

b) conceive

c) conceal

d) convey

---

59 The girl was ___ at the news of her father's death.

a) outraged

b) decimated

c) damaged

d) devastated

---

60 Even though he tried to hide it, I could see ___ his intentions from the very beginning.

a) through

b) thorough

c) true

d) throughout

---

61 My car cost a ___ $ 100,000.

a) dizzy

b) churning

c) staggering

d) daunting

---

62 The candidate made a(n) ___ attempt to destroy his rival.

a) introvert

b) cynical

c) blatant

d) overt

---

63 I was ___ by a sports car on the highway.

a) overrun

b) overdone

c) overtaken
d) overcome

---

64 Whenever someone opposed his points of view, he would ___ sharply.
a) retort
b) distort
c) deny
d) swerve

---

65 Everyone disapproved of his ___ behavior towards the teacher.
a) pliable
b) nonchalant
c) despondent
d) contemptuous

---

66 He tried hard to ___ his real feelings not to hurt his girlfriend.
a) reveal
b) conceal
c) conceive
d) dispel

---

67 The lecturer tried to speak ___ so everybody could hear him clearly.
a) laudably
b) favorably
c) distinctly
d) fervently

---

68 My teacher ___ me for trying to cheat in the test.
a) demoralized
b) escorted
c) scolded
d) unqualified

---

69 The woman ___ a headache and left the meeting.
a) feigned

b) emulated
c) started
d) intended

---

70 Only the ___ can afford to buy this luxury sports car.
a) have-nots
b) well-advised
c) well-groomed
d) well-to-do

---

71 Authorities had ___ some money for rescue operations.
a) selected
b) allocated
c) endowed
d) envisaged

---

72 His ___ death devastated his fans all over the world.
a) unduly
b) untimely
c) belated
d) subdued

---

73 It's no use talking to her. She won't change her mind. She's always so ___.
a) indecisive
b) reconciling
c) unreliable
d) uncompromising

---

74 Taking a ___ year before moving on to university could be a wonderful experience.
a) gap
b) leap
c) single
d) free

75 We can only rely on ___ sources to carry out the study.

a) despicable

b) trustworthy

c) uncommitted

d) compromising

---

76 The manager had a(n) ___ of temper when the workers said they'd go on strike.

a) tantrum

b) output

c) outcome

d) outburst

---

77 He will go out of his ___ to help his friends.

a) path

b) way

c) route

d) street

---

78 My father went ___ when he found out what I had done.

a) baffled

b) flabbergasted

c) bewildered

d) berserk

---

79 There was a cholera ___ in the city.

a) outbreak

b) onset

c) outcast

d) outcome

---

80 She has a reserved ___.

a) complexion

b) virtue

c) demeanor
d) disposition

---

81 I was a(n) ___ at that party. Everyone was younger than me.
a) outlaw
b) misfit
c) alien
d) gap

---

82 I made a(n) ___ mistake when I was preparing the lecture.
a) blunder
b) intent
c) inadequate
d) inadvertent

---

83 The principal only gave us a(n) ___ answer.
a) non-committal
b) carefree
c) exquisite
d) unaware

---

84 People need heroes to look ___, says the song.
a) up on
b) up at
c) down on
d) up to

---

85 The ___ rain never seemed to stop.
a) unrelenting
b) thick
c) tidal
d) enduring

---

86 I don't like this movie. It has too much ___ violence.
a) fortuitous

b) scenic
c) gratuitous
d) free

---

87 These twins are just so identical I could never tell them ___.
a) off
b) out
c) apart
d) aside

---

88 What I can say about her is that she's a competent actress ___.
a) through and through
b) by and large
c) all in all
d) on and off

---

89 If you intend to go camping, you should take ___ measures to prevent accidents.
a) precautionary
b) prohibitive
c) forbidding
d) prescriptive

---

90 There is rumored to be a wild animal ___ in the neighborhood.
a) in and out
b) on the run
c) on the loose
d) off track

---

91 The death ___ after the tsunami has reached 10,000 victims so far.
a) quantity
b) toll
c) tax
d) take

92 My father has taken me to ___ because I got into trouble at school.

a) task

b) work

c) job

d) duty

---

93 This poem ___ images of a Christmas night by the open fire.

a) provokes

b) conjures up

c) brings about

d) eludes

---

94 I had so much fun at the party. We danced the night ___.

a) away

b) out

c) down

d) along

---

95 Nessie is a(n) ___ creature which is said to inhabit Loch Ness, in Scotland.

a) pervasive

b) elusive

c) allusive

d) evasive

---

96 ___ should workers give interviews without our permission.

a) On account of

b) By all accounts

c) On no account

d) On that account

---

97 The swimmers are lucky to be alive. They ___ escaped a shark attack.

a) narrowly

b) closely

c) thinly
d) nearly

---

98 The teacher didn't know what to do. She was taken ___ by the students' unruly behavior.
a) away
b) down
c) aback
d) off

---

99 Eating with your mouth open is a(n) ___ of etiquette.
a) break
b) mistake
c) error
d) breach

---

100 You won't get ___ with drug trafficking. They'll catch you sooner or later.
a) away
b) down
c) off
d) over

---

101 I got so emotional at the ceremony that I was at a ___ for words.
a) lack
b) blank
c) loss
d) want

---

102 He's a very reserved, ___ man. He doesn't like to talk to anyone.
a) garrulous
b) loquacious
c) fidgety
d) withdrawn

103 He's been so negligent. He's lost his job because he's so ___.

a) undependable

b) diligent

c) independent

d) autonomous

---

104 Paul has been charged with being a(n) ___ to murder.

a) accessory

b) contributor

c) adviser

d) collaborator

---

105 I couldn't put with his ___ attitude towards me.

a) off-key

b) offside

c) off limits

d) off-hand

---

106 Paris enjoys such a reputation that it has a great deal to ___.

a) come up to

b) live up to

c) catch up on

d) come down with

---

107 You were lucky to have escaped. One day you'll tell your grandsons you lived to tell the ___.

a) tale

b) story

c) event

d) case

---

108 Has the doctor given you any ___ medicine?

a) description

b) prescription

c) receipt
d) recipe

---

109 The teacher ___ too much homework in yesterday's class.
a) ascribed
b) prescribed
c) assigned
d) assorted

---

110 I didn't know what to say because I was caught off ___.
a) guard
b) tracks
c) surprise
d) hand

---

111 ___ to their parents, the youngsters went camping in a dangerous area.
a) Unaware
b) Unbeknown
c) Innocent
d) Inadvertent

---

112 I had a(n) ___ sensation that wherever we went there was someone lurking around.
a) uncanny
b) fake
c) freak
d) loathsome

---

113 The boy was struck by a ___ bullet.
a) lost
b) astray
c) stray
d) loose

114 Dietary foods are usually so ___.

a) brand

b) trite

c) soothing

d) bland

---

115 I can't go on. I'm dead on my ___.

a) head

b) body

c) hands

d) feet

---

116 She'd been meaning to write a book, but never ___.

a) sorted it out

b) fell through

c) pulled through

d) got it together

---

117 Researchers say a scientific revolution in the fight against cancer is ___.

a) in the way

b) underway

c) underlying

d) in the way

---

118 The young singer was given a(n) ___ ovation.

a) outstanding

b) standing

c) splendid

d) stupid

---

119 I hated the meeting because of those ___ discussions.

a) elongated

b) protracted

c) lingering

d) extensive

120 During the interview I was on ___. I hope despite my nervousness, I have passed.

a) edge

b) end

c) time

d) duty

---

121 Everyone was appalled at the boss's ___ reaction to the workers' strike.

a) confrontational

b) amiable

c) flattering

d) unprepossessing

---

122 These trees ___ their leaves in the fall.

a) cast

b) shed

c) spell

d) stroll

---

123 Don't ___ a red light. It is a serious driving offense.

a) fly

b) skip

c) jump

d) move

---

124 The swimmers played ___ unaware of the danger around.

a) ridiculously

b) blissfully

c) hauntingly

d) merrily

---

125 Don't mess with the new teacher. She's so ___.

a) quick-tempered

b) organized

c) stingy
d) morose

---

126 My father went through the ___ when I told him I was pregnant.
a) ceiling
b) attic
c) roof
d) window

---

127 If you make an exception this time, you set a dangerous ___.
a) consequence
b) malpractice
c) precedent
d) precedence

---

128 Although I'm not ___ to fish, I'd rather eat red meat.
a) adverse
b) averse
c) inverse
d) reverse

---

129 "What kinds of restaurants do you prefer?"
"Any will be fine by me. I'm not ___."
a) antagonistic
b) inclined
c) particular
d) bossy

---

130 There's ___ no possibility of anyone escaping from this prison.
a) narrowly
b) roughly
c) broadly
d) virtually

131 I have (a)n ___ he will have already left work.

a) hunch

b) omen

c) punch

d) stench

---

132 We are now witnessing a(n) ___ of interest in old cinema.

a) renovation

b) reparation

c) renaissance

d) renewal

---

133 The Titanic departed on an ominous day, on its ___ voyage.

a) raid

b) maiden

c) express

d) hoax

---

134 This exotic Asian flower ___ a nasty smell.

a) gives away

b) gives off

c) sends off

d) brings about

---

135 The food was shiny and moist. It was so ___.

a) offensive

b) disgusting

c) inviting

d) nasty

---

136 Bad language is no longer a source of ___ between students and teachers.

a) intrigue

b) hatred

c) frailty

d) friction

137 Scientists usually ___ popular medicine out of hand.

a) encourage

b) dismiss

c) consider

d) think

---

138 In my work, I have a lot of deadlines to ___.

a) match

b) meet

c) encounter

d) face

---

139 My weekdays have been hectic recently. I'm rushed off my ___.

a) mind

b) legs

c) feet

d) head

---

140 The candidate was not given the opportunity because of his ___ behavior.

a) unflattering

b) flawless

c) disreputable

d) unrelenting

---

141 His enthusiasm for his studies continues ___.

a) unattainable

b) unabated

c) unabashed

d) untenable

---

142 Understanding our human condition on earth is an eternal ___.

a) conundrum

b) grind

c) trifle
d) matter

---

143 He returned the T-shirt to the store because it had a ___ in the pattern.
a) deficiency
b) dent
c) bump
d) deformity

---

144 Don't be so ___. There are many religious leaders who want to mislead us.
a) believable
b) credulous
c) ingenious
d) comprehensive

---

145 The tribe offered a ceremony to ___ their gods' fury.
a) suffocate
b) smother
c) drawn
d) appease

---

146 Don't ___ it out on me, it was your own fault.
a) get
b) have
c) take
d) make

---

147 Our opinions are generally ___, but this time I admit you're right.
a) discrete
b) interchangeable
c) divergent
d) congruent

148 Advertisements shouldn't encourage children to ___ parents to buy them things they don't need.

a) blunder
b) abhor
c) loathe
d) pester

---

149 I wish you would stop ___ your nose, it drives me crazy.

a) lifting
b) licking
c) biting
d) picking

---

150 I agree that the movie is good, but I think people's opinions about it are a bit ___.

a) far-fetched
b) understated
c) unappreciative
d) overrated

---

151 If you don't want your friends to turn their backs on you, you'll have to change your ___.

a) ways
b) means
c) paths
d) manners

---

152 I've had a painkiller, but it must be ___. I have a headache.

a) running out
b) running low
c) wearing out
d) wearing off

153 Don't ___ your feelings. Show them openly and you'll feel better.

a) bottle up

b) let down

c) put away

d) lay down

---

154 He was ___ against teasing the dog, but he would not listen.

a) adverted

b) advised

c) advertised

d) repelled

---

155 The play was enacted with ___ skill.

a) admonitory

b) deliberate

c) consummate

d) accredited

---

156 With some gentle ___, we managed to make him give the secret away.

a) hoax

b) coaxing

c) dexterity

d) attrition

---

157 After constant bullying at school, the student felt miserable and ___.

a) inadequate

b) inappropriate

c) inaccurate

d) inopportune

---

158 I ___ you to help me with this. Don't disappoint me!

a) get to

b) view on

c) count on

d) go to

159 The candidate was so edgy and ___ about the job interview.
a) apprehensive
b) unabridged
c) mystified
d) ecstatic

---

160 All students, ___ of their social backgrounds, receive equal treatment in this school.
a) irrespective
b) despite
c) in spite
d) regarding

---

161 Advertisements shouldn't cause any kind of offense on the ___ of sexuality.
a) grounds
b) basis
c) terms
d) means

---

162 The accuser, under ___, gave strong evidence against the defendant.
a) solemnity
b) oath
c) swearing
d) promise

---

163 My teacher said my essay was too ___ .
a) childish
b) infant
c) pedestrian
d) poor

---

164 My mother is so intelligent. She always gives me ___ advice when I'm in trouble.
a) judicial

b) judicious
c) prejudiced
d) prejudicial

---

165 They threw a lavish party to ___ the writer's new book.
a) publicize
b) divulge
c) spread
d) exploit

---

166 It is not widely accepted that death penalty would act as a(n) ___ to crime.
a) repentance
b) deterrent
c) infringement
d) defensive

---

167 There's only a ___ possibility that he will win the race.
a) fat
b) thin
c) faint
d) small

---

168 A party on Saturday? Sorry, I have a ___. My boyfriend is taking me out.
a) counterpart
b) contrivance
c) restraint
d) conflict

---

169 I'd like to apologize to you all on ___ of my supervisor.
a) person
b) charge
c) behalf
d) place

170 The movie made the audience cry, it was so ___ to getting emotional.

a) prone
b) conductive
c) conducive
d) adequate

---

171 The student's ___ attitude towards the teacher led to his being expelled.

a) obdurate
b) obstinate
c) frail
d) recalcitrant

---

172 There were many famous painters in the Renaissance, but Da Vinci ___ them all.

a) outdated
b) outlived
c) outmoded
d) outshone

---

173 I'll pursue my goals, come what ___.

a) comes
b) may
c) will
d) happens

---

174 You can count on me. I'm on your ___.

a) side
b) way
c) right
d) view

---

175 I just couldn't make up my ___ whether or not I'd go to the party.

a) head
b) thought

c) mind
d) decision

---

176 I'd like to ___ you company, but unfortunately I have to leave.
a) do
b) make
c) keep
d) give

---

177 I make a ___ of giving back homework to my students as soon as possible.
a) question
b) point
c) matter
d) preoccupation

---

178 Mr. Johnson is well known for his ___. He is extremely concerned about saving his money.
a) sagacity
b) mendacity
c) acrimony
d) parsimony

---

179 I was suddenly taken by a(n) ___ of resentment.
a) surge
b) instance
c) instant
d) upsurge

---

180 Why are you always so ___? I'd be happy if you were more outgoing.
a) lonely
b) withdrawn
c) retrieved
d) contrived

181 All Miss Helena's students like her because she is so ___.

a) understandable

b) comprehensive

c) undependable

d) sympathetic

---

182 The company seeks a(n) ___ and committed professional.

a) affluent

b) imminent

c) outstanding

d) effluent

---

183 I'm still fighting off the flu, but I'm ___. I'm already getting better.

a) on the loose

b) on the mend

c) off road

d) safe and sound

---

184 His friends called him a bookworm because of his ___ appetite for books.

a) enormous

b) gigantic

c) voracious

d) crazy

---

185 I just have no idea how we are going to ___ with this situation.

a) meet

b) resolve

c) content

d) contend

---

186 The boastful fighter had to eat humble ___ when he lost the championship.

a) pie

b) bread

c) food

d) apple

187 Examples of foul language ___ in this movie.
a) collect
b) amount
c) abound
d) amass

---

188 ___ work is approaching its end with the help of modern technology.
a) Backbreaking
b) Scorching
c) Overbearing
d) Remunerated

---

189 Scientists still cannot ___ what will happen to the research results.
a) procrastinate
b) prognosticate
c) prescribe
d) estimate

---

190 He's not trustworthy. I take everything he says with a pinch of ___.
a) doubt
b) salt
c) sand
d) disbelief

---

191 I was browsing through an old book when I came ___ this picture.
a) up with
b) in for
c) down with
d) across

---

192 The teacher told me to do a ___ review of my essay to check it for accuracy.
a) throughout
b) thorough

c) thoroughly
d) through

---

193 Don't relax on your ___ just because you're at home. Always be polite!
a) moods
b) behavior
c) education
d) manners

---

194 Handing in your final term paper is ___.
a) compulsory
b) demanding
c) demanded
d) derogatory

---

195 We cannot ___ any kind of prejudice in this company.
a) bias
b) deport
c) condone
d) coax

---

196 The email we received from the bank was only a ___.
a) hoax
b) myth
c) delusion
d) play

---

197 My employees are always ___ me to get some advantage. I know it's not sincere.
a) pestering
b) fostering
c) egging
d) flattering

198 This novel's plot is so ___. It's based on a lot of clichéd ideas.

a) uncommon

b) uninviting

c) hackneyed

d) trifle

---

199 He was charged with being a(n) ___ to crime. He was not directly involved in it.

a) supportive

b) accessory

c) supporting

d) accidental

---

200 It's getting late. I must be on my ___ now.

a) path

b) route

c) way

d) road

KEY TO FINAL VOCABULARY REVIEW

1 B) (= interpretation, performance)
2 B) (= scarcity, reduction)
3 D) "Beauty is in the eye of the beholder" is an idiom. It means beauty is a relative concept. "Beholder" is the one who "beholds" (= "look at", "see").
4 A) (= money paid to leave jail until you are summoned to appear in court)
5 D) (= food used to attract fish. Idiom: "you are coaxed into taking part in a quarrel")
6 A) (= recognized)
7 C) (= waiting for)
8 B) If you say you have something <u>thanks to</u> something else, you have something <u>because of</u> something else.
9 C) (= determine, establish)
10 A) (= having nothing to do)
11 C) (= a period of time)
12 D) An "only child" has no siblings.
13 B) (= desired, craved)
14 D) (= empty)
15 A) (= deterrent, discouragement)
16 D) (= banish, repel)
17 A) (= disturbing, troublesome)
18 D) (= great happiness)
19 D) (= tempt, lure)
20 A) (= excused from payment)
21 B) (= expulsion)
22 A) (= to not need anybody else's help)
23 A) Idiom
24 A) (= arrogant)
25 D) (= cultivated, educated)
26 B) (= distant)

27 C) (= frenetic, frenzied, full of activity)
28 B) (= it was a disappointment)
29 D) (= keeping himself away from people)
30 A) (= encounter something unpleasant)
31 C) (= overcome)
32 B) (= outspoken, unrestrained)
33 C) (= to lose control because of excitement)
34 A) (= received)
35 A) (= don't be angry)
36 C) (= weak)
37 A) (= to feel sick)
38 D) (= people who have a lot in common stay in the same groups)
39 C) (= lose out)
40 A) (= ignore, abandon)
41 D) (= dead or injured victims)
42 B) (= you were cheated financially)
43 A) (= caused)
44 C) (= tolerate)
45 A) (= sociable)
46 D) (= respectful)
47 C) (= finally)
48 A) (= difficult, hard)
49 B) (= look away)
50 D) (= postponed)
51 A) (= only just manage financially because you do not have enough money)
52 C) (= in agreement with)
53 A) (= aggressive)
54 D) (= not having a job or a place to stay)
55 B (= something useful)
56 A) (= practicable, that is able to be done)
57 C) (= recuperate)
58 B) (= imagine, believe)
59 D) (= shocked, upset)

60 A) (= realize, perceive)
61 C) (= surprising, astounding)
62 C) (= obvious) collocation pattern
63 C) (= passed)
64 A) (= answer snappily)
65 D) (= disdainful, disrespectful)
66 B) (= hide)
67 C) (= clearly)
68 C) (= tell off, rebuke)
69 A) (= pretend)
70 D) (= the rich; the poor are the "have-nots")
71 B (= assign, designate)
72 B) (= happening too early)
73 D) (= intransigent, inflexible)
74 B) (= a year without studying before you move on to college)
75 B) (= reliable, dependable)
76 D) (= explosion)
77 B) (= to do whatever you can to help)
78 D) (= he got furious.)
79 A) (= a surge)
80 C) (= behavior)
81 B) (= unsuited to the occasion)
82 D) (= unintentional)
83 A) (= evasive, vague)
84 D) (= admire, follow as models)
85 A) (= never ceasing)
86 C) (= uncalled for, futile)
87 C) (= distinguish, tell the difference)
88 A) (= complete, consummate)
89 A) (= done to avoid danger or problems)
90 C) If an animal is *on the loose*, it has escaped from where it was kept (a zoo, for example) and has not been recaptured yet. You can also use the expression to talk about people: "The murderous maniacal remains on the loose."

91 B) (= the number of)
92 A) (= tell off, reprimand)
93 B) (= evoke, bring to mind)
94 A) If you "do something the night away", you do it for the whole night.
95 B) An "elusive animal" is one which is difficult to be seen.
96 C) (= under no circumstances)
97 A) collocation pattern
98 C) (= surprised)
99 D) (= failure to observe a rule)
100 A) (= escape punishment)
101 C) (= speechless, not knowing what to say)
102 D) (= introverted)
103 (= someone you cannot rely on or count on)
104 A) (= accomplice, partner in crime)
105 D) (= rude)
106 B) (= fulfill)
107 A) (= survive and be able to talk about it later)
108 B) (= instructions for the use of medicine)
109 C) (= designated)
110 A) (= be caught unawares, by surprise)
111 B) (= without the knowledge of someone) Note: also "unbeknownst"
112 A) (= strange, mysterious)
113 C) A "stray bullet" deviates from the intended course and strikes a person or thing it was not aimed at.
114 D) (= tasteless, insipid)
115 D) (= worn out, exhausted)
116 D) (= never really took positive action to do it)
117 B) (= in progress)
118 B) (= applaud enthusiastically)
119 B) (= lasting for a long time)
120 A) (= nervous, anxious)
121 A) (= argumentative; react angrily, cause arguments)
122 B) (= trees that lose their leaves in autumn)
123 C) (= to not stop at a red light)

124 B) (= perfect happiness). “Blissfully” often collocates with “happy”, “ignorant” and “unaware”.
125 A) If someone is “quick-tempered”, they get angry easily.
126 C) (= lose your temper)
127 C) “To set a precedent” for an action or event means that it happened before and will be used as argument for doing it again later on.
128 B) (= strongly opposed to)
129 C) If you are not particular, you’ll be happy with any choice.
130 D) (= almost)
131 A) (= an idea based on a feeling and for which there’s no evidence)
132 C) (= a new development)
133 B) (= inaugural)
134 B) (= emit)
135 C) (= attractive, encouraging)
136 D) (= animosity, conflict)
137 B) (= disregard without any serious consideration)
138 B) (= to meet a deadline)
139 C) (= very busy)
140 C) (= not enjoying a good reputation)
141 B) (= continuing without losing intensity)
142 A) (= riddle)
143 D) (= spoiled) The word is frequently more associated with the body.
144 B) (= ingenuous, willing to believe without thinking critically)
145 D) (= quell, pacify)
146 C) (= put the blame on someone)
147 C) (= conflicting, different)
148 D) (= bother, harass)
149 D) (= to remove something from your nose using your fingers)
150 D) (= place more value on something than it really deserves)
151 A) (= change your behavior) collocation pattern
152 D) (= lose effects)
153 A) (= to refuse to talk about your feelings)
154 B) (= warned)
155 C) (= flawless, complete, impeccable)

156 B) (= to obtain something by gently persuading someone)
157 A) If you "feel inadequate", you think you're not good enough.
158 C) (= rely on)
159 A) (= nervous, anxious) Also note: "to feel on edge"
160 A) (= regardless of)
161 A) (= based on)
162 B) (= under the commitment of telling the truth in a court of law)
163 C) (= commonplace, simplistic)
164 B) (= wise) Please note: "judicial" is related to "justice".
165 A) (= make known to the public) Note: "divulge" cannot be used in this sense.
166 B) (= disincentive)
167 C) If you talk about a "faint possibility", it means that there's virtually no possibility (this is a collocation pattern). You can also say "a remote possibility". If there are more possibilities of something happening, then they are "strong", "real" or "distinct" possibilities.
168 D) If you say "I have a conflict", it's because you've previously arranged to something, when somebody invites you to do something else.
169 C) When you do something "on someone's behalf", you do it as if you were a representative of that person.
170 C) (= appropriate for this end)
171 D) (= willfully disobedient)
172 D) (= outclass, made someone lose in importance)
173 B) (= It doesn't matter what I'll have to face)
174 A) (= You have my support)
175 C) (= make a decision)
176 C) Collocation pattern
177 B) If you make a point of doing something, it means that it is extremely important for you.
178 D) (= stinginess)
179 A) If you are "overcome" or "taken" by a certain feeling, you experience it suddenly. Note: even though "upsurge" and "surge" are synonyms, this is a collocation pattern.
180 B) (= introverted)

181 D (= kind, understanding)

182 C) If you are "outstanding" (the idea comes from the verb "to stand out", that is, "to make it noticeable"), everyone notices how good you are at something.

183 B (= to recover from an illness or injury)

184 C) (= voracious, eager, avid)

185 D) (= deal with)

186 A) (idiom = to admit you've done something wrong and apologize for it)

187 C) (= exist in large numbers) Note: "abound" is a verb. The related noun is "abundance".

188 A) "Backbreaking work " (that is, work that "breaks your back") is very hard work.

189 B) (= foretell, predict)

190 B) (Idiom) If you "take something with a pinch of salt", you are not completely sure whether you could believe it or not.

191 D) (= find something unexpectedly)

192 B) (= careful, complete, detailed) A useful word that expresses the same idea is *exhaustive:* "The teacher told me to carry out an exhaustive piece of research..."

193 D) Please note: "education" has to do with schooling. An "uneducated" person may have not attended school and still be "polite".

194 A) (= It is an obligation to do it.)

195 C) (= accept)

196 A) (= a trick)

197 D) (= exaggerated praise)

198 C) (= banal, pedestrian, trite)

199 B) (= accomplice)

200 C) (= I must leave now.)

EXTRAS A

TRUE FRIENDS

True friends can be easily recognized. However, it is necessary to bring them to attention so that you can use them, as we tend to look at them as if they were ***false friends***. Below you have some essential ***true friends*** (or their true friend synonyms and shades of meaning). They've been listed alphabetically so you can look them up easily in a dictionary, if necessary.

A, C

assiduous (= diligent)
calamity (= disaster)
capitulate (= surrender, yield)
cede (= concede)
chronic (= persistent)
commence (= begin)
compatible (= consistent, consonant)
conscript (= draftee)
contentious (= argumentative)

D

delegate (v) (= entrust) (as a noun = representative)
deleterious (= destructive, detrimental)
deliberate (= intentional)
discord (= conflict)
disparity (= discrepancy)
dissension (= discord, disagreement)
diverge (= disagree)
domicile (= abode)

E, F

evasive (= non-committal)

exasperation (= irritation, vexation)
exile (= deportee)
façade (= misleading outward appearance)
foment (= incite)
frugal (= thrifty)

I

imbecile (= idiot)
immense (= enormous)
impede (= hinder)
implore (= beg)
improvise (= perform without previous preparation)
incisive (= clear, decisive)
indigent (= the poor)
indiscriminate (= random, arbitrary)
inevitable (= unavoidable)
infringe (= violate, contravene)
insinuate (= imply)
intimidate (= subdue, threaten)

M, O, P

molest (= abuse sexually)
omniscient (= knowing everything)
prerogative (= right, privilege)
prestige (= reputation)
procrastinate (= delay, postpone)
prodigy (= genius, wonder)
propensity (= inclination)
protocol (= etiquette) (see the expression "minor breaches of protocol")

R, S

recuperate (= recover)
redundant (= surplus)
retaliate (= repay an injury in return)

stereotype (= conventional or hackneyed)
subjugate (= oppress, dominate)
subterfuge (= deceit, deception)
subtle (= understated, not obvious)
subvert (= undermine, destabilize)
succinct (= brief)
suffocate (= smother, asphyxiate)
surreptitious (= stealthy, furtive)

T, V

temperamental (= moody)
tribulation (= trouble, suffering)
tyrannical (= imperious)
vehement (= passionate, ardent)
vicarious (= experienced indirectly, in the imagination)

EXTRAS B

FALSE FRIENDS

Some essential **false friends** (with current main use)

A

abort = cancelar; ***aborto*** (de feto) ➢ miscarriage
actually = na verdade; ***atualmente*** ➢ nowadays
adept = hábil; adepto, ***seguidor*** ➢ follower
advice = counsel; ***aviso*** ➢ warning
agenda = pauta; ***caderno*** (de endereços) ➢ address book
amass = juntar; ***amassar*** (por exemplo, papel) ➢ crumple
argument = discussão (briga); ***discussão*** (de ideias) ➢ discussion

C

candid = franco, honesto; ***cândido*** (ingênuo) ➢ naive
casualty = vítima, feridos (de acidente); ***casualidade*** ➢ chance, accident
college = faculdade; ***colégio*** ➢ high school (equivalente ao Ensino Médio)
compass = bússola (mas também ➢ *compasso*, instrumento para traçar círculos)
comprehensive = completo, abrangente; ***compreensivo*** ➢ understanding, sympathetic
compromise = transigência; ***compromisso*** ➢ appointment
convict = prisioneiro; ***convicto*** ➢ certain, convinced
costume = fantasia, traje típico; ***costume*** (hábito) ➢ custom

D, E

deception = cilada, trapaça; ***decepção*** ➢ disappointment
ecstatic = extasiado; ***estático*** ➢ static
educated = culto, que tem escolaridade formal; ***educado*** ➢ polite
engrossed = absorto, envolvido; ***engrossar*** (líquido) ➢ thicken
eventual = final; ***eventual*** (ocasional) ➢ occasional

eventually = finalmente, por fim; ***eventualmente*** (às vezes, ocasionalmente) ➢ occasionally
excited = agitado, alvoroçado; ***excitado*** (sexualmente) ➢ (sexually) aroused
exit = saída; ***êxito*** ➢ success
exquisite = delicado, primoroso; ***esquisito*** ➢ odd, weird

F, G
fabric = tecido, pano; ***fábrica*** ➢ factory
facilities = instalações, acomodações; ***facilidade*** ➢ easiness
graphic = explícito (graphic violence), mas também *gráfico*

I
indigenous = nativo, natural, autóctone; ***indígena*** ➢ indian, native
ingenious = engenhoso, hábil; ***ingênuo*** ➢ ingenuous, naïve

L, M
legend = lenda; ***legenda*** (de filme) ➢ caption, subtitle
malice = maldade, premeditação; ***malícia*** (licenciosidade) ➢ lewdness, lechery

N, P
novel = romance, novela (gênero literário); ***novela*** (televisiva) ➢ soap opera
particular = exigente; ***particular*** (propriedade) ➢ private
pretend = fingir; ***pretender*** ➢ intend

R, S
romance = paixão, romantismo; ***romance*** (gênero literário) ➢ novel
resume = retomar, recomeçar; ***resumir*** ➢ sum up, summarize
sensible = sensato, racional; ***sensível*** ➢ sensitive
support = apoiar; ***suportar*** (tolerar) ➢ stand, tolerate
sympathetic = favorável; ***simpático*** ➢ nice, friendly

T, U
terrific = fantástico; ***terrível*** ➢ terrible

travesty = farsa, paródia, aberração; ***travesti*** ➢ transvestite, cross dresser
utlimately = em última análise, em última instância; ***ultimamente*** ➢ recently

EXTRAS C

VERB + NOUN COLLOCATIONS

Useful collocations with similar/literal use in Portuguese

The following collocations are generally easily recognizable, but they need to be brought to attention as we tend dismiss collocations which are translated literally (or almost literally) from Portuguese into English.

acknowledge receipt of (a letter) (= acusar o recebimento de uma carta)
adopt a custom
air your views (the same as "express")
alleviate pain/suffering
bear false witness (against someone) (= prestar falso testemunho)
bear a grudge (against someone)
bear fruit
break your word
bury yourself on your books
carry something too far
catch a cold/fire
change your mind
cross someone's path
cultivate friendship
cut the Gordian Knot (= cortar o Nó Górdio)
draw the line at
eat your words
exercise authority
fill a vacancy
form an opinion
gain time
give cause for complaint
hold your breath

keep a secret/house/company (= manter segredo, cuidar da casa, fazer companhia)
lend a hand
lose your temper/your head
pay someone a visit
pay someone back in his/their own coin (= pagar na mesma moeda)
raise an objection
read someone's mind/thoughts
resist an enemy
see eye to eye (= não se combinar)
seize an opportunity
set an example (= dar exemplo)
show your teeth (start behaving aggressively) (= mostrar as unhas)
spread rumors
support a football team (show it is your favorite) (= torcer para um time)
take measures
take the liberty (of doing something) (= tomar a liberdade de fazer algo)
throw cold water (on an idea)
withdraw your remarks (retract) (= retirar suas palavras, retratar-se)

EXTRAS D

ADVERBIAL IDIOMATIC PHRASES

These need to be brought to attention because they're not easily recognizable as the individual words do not make sense separately, but as a whole.

By the by = by the way
By the by, did you hear Sally's just gotten married?

By and large = on the whole
By and large, the plan has been a success.

Firstly and foremost = in the first place
Firstly and foremost, I'd like to say...

Here and there = in various places
There were animals ***here and there*** all over the place.

Neither here nor there = irrelevant
Don't worry about your minor mistakes. It's ***neither here nor there***.

Now and again = occasionally (or: ***now and then***)
Now and again I think of moving to the countryside.

On and off (also ***off and on***) = continually
It's been snowing ***on and off*** all day.

Once and for all = for the last time, definitely
I'm telling you ***once and for all*** that I will keep my promise.

Out and out = completely
His performance in the test was an ***out and out*** disaster.

Through and through = completely ("de cabo a rabo")

I'm against his plans ***through and through***.

up and about = standing on your feet again (after recuperating from an illness)

He's ***up and about*** now that he's recovered from a surgery.

up and up = improving

Customer's confidence in our business is ***up and up*** again.

EXTRAS E

PREPOSITIONAL IDIOMATIC PHRASES

These phrases are usually easily recognizable because there is a noun in the phrase around which meaning is concentrated.

On account of (= because of)
He was fired ***on account of*** his involvement in the political scandal.

On behalf of (= as someone's representative) (= em nome de)
"I would like to thank you all ***on behalf of*** the captain of this flight for flying with us," said the flight attendant.
(Or: = because of or for someone) (= por minha causa)
Please, don't go to any trouble ***on behalf of*** me. (or: "... any trouble ***on my account***.")

In charge of (= under the responsibility of)
Do you know who's ***in charge of*** administering the examinations?

In compliance with (= in accordance to)
All the students are expected to behave ***in compliance with*** the school's rules.

In exchange for (= give something and receive something else)
I lent him the book ***in exchange for*** his help to write my paper.

At the expense of (= to the detriment of)
Progress cannot come ***at the expense of*** nature destruction.

With an eye to (= with the purpose of, also: *with a view to*)
I''m working hard ***with an eye to*** studying in a prestigious university.

In lieu of (= instead of; formal)

The teacher assigned us a painstaking task ***in lieu of*** the final examinations.

By means of (= using a particular method or system)

He managed to enter university ***by means of*** careful study and hard work.

under the pretense of (= making people believe what is not true)

The student told the teacher he had to leave ***under the pretense of*** a headache.

In (the) pursuit of (= find something in a determined way)

In the pursuit of his goals, he applied himself diligently to his studies.

With recourse to (= using or doing something) (= com recurso a, por meio de)

The dangerous riots were only controlled ***with recourse to*** police intervention.

For the sake of (= for the good of) (= por zelo ao nome de)

The strikers withdrew their decision ***for the sake of*** the company's good reputation.

In spite of (= despite, without being prevented by something)

In spite of his poor health, he succeeded in completing his work in due time.

As a token of (= something that represents a feeling) (= como prova, sinal, etc.)

Please accept this gift ***as a (small) token*** of our friendship.

By virtue of (= because of)

The student was withdrawn from school ***by virtue of*** his bad behavior.

In the wake of (= as a result of; especially something bad)

Destruction followed ***in the wake of*** the tornadoes which swept the region.

Extras F

PREPOSITIONAL PHRASES (Similar in form but different in meaning)

These need to be brought to attention because their similarity may be a pitfall, even when the difference is subtle.

in case of (= in the event of) / ***in the case of*** (= regarding)

In case of emergency, don't hesitate to call us.

All students did well in the test, but ***in the case of John's***, he failed dismally.

in (the) face of (= in the presence of) / ***on the face of it*** (= "à primeira vista", "ao que parece")

In face of danger, he showed courage and determination.

'***On the face of it***, we might be able to come up with a solution soon.

for fear of (= because of fear) / ***in fear of*** (= anxious for the safety of)

I keep most of my money at the bank ***for fear of*** our home being broken into.

He cut down on smoking ***in fear of*** his health.

by the name of (= named, with the name) / ***in the name of*** (= for the love of)

A man ***by the name of*** Jason got killed mysteriously in a campsite last night.

Many crimes have been committed ***in the name of*** faith in religion.

at the point of (= approaching a state) / ***on the point of*** (= about to do, on the verge of)

The old dog's health was so poor that it was ***at the point of*** death.

I was ***on the point of*** leaving when the telephone rang.

with regard to (considering) / ***out of regard for*** (= because of respect/ consideration for)

With regard to the safety of the students, the school is going to invest in security.

The student was awarded an honors certificate ***out of regard*** for his dedication.

at the sight of (= when seeing) / ***in the sight of*** (= from the point of view)

She cried ***at the sight of*** the destruction caused by the tornado.

In the sight of law, you're guilty, even if you're forgivable from the view of religion.

at the time of (= at a particular point of time) / ***in time of*** (= at a general time)

I survived the explosion because I wasn't home ***at the time of*** the explosion.

In time of tragedies and need, we should be grateful for whatever we have left.

in view of (= regarding) / ***with a view to*** (= with the purpose of, *with an eye to*

In view of my poor grades, I decided to apply myself harder to my studies.

I had to work harder and harder ***with a view to*** getting a promotion.

Note: in the phrase "***with a view/an eye to***", ***to*** is a preposition; therefore it should be followed by the gerund.

for want of (= because of the lack of) / ***in want of*** (= in need of)

The stray dog died miserably in the streets ***for want of*** food.

I'm badly ***in want of*** new clothes, but I can't afford to buy any now.

EXTRAS 9

IDIOMATIC USES OF COMMON NOUNS AND ADJECTIVES

Here are some curious idiomatic uses of some common nouns and adjectives as the main word in idiomatic expressions which you might want to look up in a dictionary. Some of them have been translated into Portuguese:

dead

a *dead* wire, to be *dead* tired, to stop *dead*, to be *dead* drunk, a *dead* end, to meet a dead*line* (= cumprir prazos), *dead* and gone (or *dead* and buried)

flat

a *flat* tire, to be *flat* broke (= "quebrado", sem dinheiro)

good

good works, to give someone a *good* talking to, a *good* deal of, a *good* many, as *good* as gold, to hold *good* (= estar de pé, estar valendo), to make *good*, for *good*, for your own *good*, *good* riddance (= Já vai tarde!)

hard

hard times, *hard* words, to be *hard* of hearing, to be *hard* pressed, to be/play *hard* to please, to be *hard* up

high

to be in *high* spirits, to be *high*, to be left *high* and dry (= estar na pior), to be *high-handed*

poor

a *poor* excuse, *poor* work, to be in *poor* health, to have a *poor* opinion of (also: to do *poorly*)

short
to feel *short-changed* (= ser lesado, enganado) *short*-change , to be *short* of money, to be *short* with someone, to cut a long story *short*, *short* temper (= to have a short fuse, "pavio curto"), in *short*, *short* of

thick
to go through *thick* and thin (= na alegria e na tristeza, venha o que vier)

thin
vanish into *thin* air

end
to make (both) *ends* meet (= dar conta das despesas), on *end*, to no *end*, *end* up

line
to draw the *line*, to drop a *line*, to toe the *line*

mind
to be in two *minds* (= estar indeciso), to be of the same *mind*, to change your *mind*, to give someone a piece of your *mind*, to have half a *mind* to do something, to bear in *mind*, speak your *mind*, to my *mind*

point
to be beside the *point*, to be on the *point* of, straight to the *point*, miss your *point*, to see the *point*, to make a *point* of doing something (= fazer questão de algo), a case in *point*, there's no *point* in

way
to be in the *way*, to get something under*way* , to go out of your *way* (= não medir esforços), to go your own *way*, to have a *way* with (= ter jeito/ habilidade com), to mend your *ways*

word

big *words*, to be *word* perfect, to be as good as your *word* (= ser uma pessoa de palavra), to break your *word*, to go back on your *word*, to eat your *words*, to get a *word* in edgeways, give your *word*, to have a *word* with someone, by *word* of mouth, mark my *words*, a play upon *words* (= trocadilho)

world

to mean the *world*, to feel on top of the *world*, out of this *world*, to come down in the *world* (= estar arruinado)

EXTRAS H

ESSENTIAL HIGH-INTERMEDIATE/ADVANCED LEVEL PHRASAL VERBS

As you are a high-intermediate or an advanced learner, we'll not provide detailed explanation on phrasal verbs, because you're already familiar with many of them. In the list below, we have used ***sb*** and ***sth*** to mean ***somebody*** and ***something***, respectively. Where a phrasal verb is *separable*, we have shown this by adding *sb* and *sth* to help you. Some of the verbs given here may have other meanings.

add up: make sense » Only now do the facts of the investigation begin to ***add up***.

answer back: return a rebuke rudely » Don't ***answer back***. I'm your mother and I'm talking to you.

answer for: take responsibility » You're mature enough to ***answer for*** your actions.

argue sb down: defeat through argument » I never seem to be able to ***argue*** *my daughter* ***down***. She's much more assertive than me.

ask sb after: inquire about a person's well-being » I was talking to your ex-husband yesterday and he ***asked*** *me* ***after*** you.

back out of: take back a promise » Please don't ***back out of*** your support now. We'd be ruined!

bank on: rely on » I wouldn't ***bank on*** his help if I were you. He's not a reliable person.

bargain for: expect » Receiving support from the manager was more than I had ***bargained for***.

be down on: be critical of » My mother's ***been down*** on me since I lost that job opportunity.

be in for: be likely to get » You ***are in for*** trouble if you don't study harder. Tests will be hard.

be in on: be informed about » I thought you ***were in on*** the plan. I'll tell you what I know.

bear out: support, confirm » The evidence collected ***bore out*** all the suspicions against him.

bear up: carry on in spite of difficulty » I can't imagine how we is ***bearing up*** after his father's death.

break in: interrupt » The teacher hated it when students would ***break in*** (on) the explanation with their silly jokes.

bring about: cause to happen » Scientific development has ***brought about*** improvements in treatments against several diseases.

bring sb down: cause defeat » Your involvement in this scandal will ***bring*** *the candidate* ***down*** at the election.

brush sth aside: dismiss out of hand, reject » When I told him what I had in mind I was so disappointed. He simply ***brushed*** *my idea* ***aside***.

brush up (on): improve by reviewing » It's extremely advisable to ***brush up*** (on) your English before you sign up for the exam.

buy sb off: pay to protect your own interest » I'll have to ***buy*** *the competitors* ***off***. I can't afford to lose now.

call for: demand, require » The challenge ***calls for*** an intelligent, bold person.

call sth off: cancel » We'll have to ***call*** *the meeting* ***off*** if the manager doesn't confirm his presence.

carry out: fulfill » We were expected to ***carry out*** our studies with unremitting application.

catch up with: get up to date » You need to ***catch up with*** the latest news urgently.

come across: meet by chance » I ***came across*** Mike at the party yesterday. We hadn't seen each other for quite a long time.

come down on: criticize » The newspapers reviewers are ***coming down*** heavily ***on*** the new book.

count sb in: include » I have a plan to defeat competitors. I hope I can ***count*** *you* ***in.***

count sb out: exclude, not consider » You'd better ***count*** *me* ***out***. I can't take part in your plan.

cut down (on): reduce » If you don't ***cut down*** (on) chocolate you'll end up like a fat whale.

do away with: abolish » Has capital punishment ***been done away with*** in your country?

do up: renovate, improve the appearance » I'm having my house ***done up*** by experienced decorators.

do without: manage without, forgo » I wish I could ***do without*** a car. Fuel and parking are so expensive nowadays.

dress up: dress formally or smartly » Everyone is expected to ***dress up*** for the formal reception.

dress down: dress casually » On Fridays we are allowed to ***dress down*** for work.

drive at: try to say, mean, imply » What are you ***driving at***? I can't understand you clearly.

drop by: pay a casual visit » Why don't you ***drop by*** and have lunch with us when you're around?

ease off: decrease tension » You need to ***ease off***, or else you'll end up having a heart attack.

ease up: lose intensity » It's been raining heavily, but it's beginning to ***ease up*** now.

face up to: accept, confront » He had to ***face up to*** the consequences of his irresponsibility.

fall back on: use as reserve » I have some savings which I can ***fall back on*** in times of trouble.

fall out with: quarrel with » She ***fell out with*** her mother and didn't speak to her for years.

fall through: fail to happen » Our plans to travel ***fell through*** because a landslide blocked the interstate.

fight sth off: defeat » I still haven't recovered from the flu. I'm still ***fighting*** *it* ***off***.

finish with: end a relationship » I've ***finished with*** my boyfriend because he was always belittling me.

follow through: continue to the end » I'll ***follow through*** with my plans until I get what I want.

get away with: escape reprimand or punishment » Be prepared. The teacher won't let you ***get way with*** cheating.

get by: manage » I can't help you. Unfortunately, you'll have to ***get by*** on your own.

get down to: start working seriously » It's time we ***got down to*** our work and finished it.

get on:
1. make progress » How are you ***getting on*** in your new job?
2. have a good relationship with (= get along) » I don't ***get on*** well with my mother.

get over:
1. overcome, surmount » Has Peter ***gotten over*** his frustration yet?
2. recover from an illness » My mother is in hospital ***getting over*** an unsuccessful surgery.

get round: evade » Don't try to ***get round*** your duties. Sooner or later, you'll get into trouble.

give sb/sth away: betray, reveal (for example, a secret) » I beg you. Don't ***give*** *me* ***away***. If I get caught, they'll fire me. You can't ***give*** *my secrets* ***away***.

give out: use up » The gas ***gave out*** when we were approaching the destination.

go about: walk about (figuratively: be friends with) » Is Sarah still ***going about*** with those weird friends of hers?

go through with: complete (see *follow through* above) » Even though it's hard, I'll ***go through with*** our deal, I promise you.

have sb down: invite to your house » We're ***having*** *some friends* ***down*** for a barbecue on the weekend. Would you like to come?

have sb on: trick » I wish you'd stop ***having*** *me* ***on***. I'm fed up with your lies.

hold on: wait » If you'll ***hold on*** a second, the manager will be with you momentarily.

keep sb in: detain after class as punishment » "If you don't behave yourselves, I'll ***keep*** *you* ***in*** for a whole week," said the teacher threateningly.

keep on at sb (about *sth*): pester, annoy » I wish you wouldn't ***keep on*** *at me* about the fender-bender. It wasn't my fault.

keep up: continue doing » You're doing well. ***Keep up*** the good work!

let sb off: not punish » You're always ***letting*** *him* ***off*** far too lightly, that's why he's so spoiled.

live sth down: get ignored, forgotten » Don't worry. All this gossip going around about you will be ***lived down*** soon.

live up to sth: maintain a standard expected of you » I hope I'll be able to ***live up to*** the expectations of my teachers and my own expectations as well.

look down on: consider inferior » My boss doesn't offer us any words of praise. On the contrary, he always ***looks down on*** us as if we were nothing.

look up: improve » The weather is ***looking up*** at last. We'll be able to go to the beach.

look up to: admire » Children always need an adult to ***look up to***.

make sb out: understand » I can't ***make*** *you* ***out***, Peter. You're always changing your mind!

make up for: compensate » I haven't read a book for ages, so I'll try to ***make up for*** this in my free time now.

make (it) up to: do something to show you regret hurting people » Sorry for what I've done to you. I'll ***make it up*** to you somehow.

pass for: be wrongly thought to be » You'd ***pass for*** an American because of your perfect English.

pick on: single out for criticism » If anything goes wrong in classroom, teachers always ***pick on*** me as a scapegoat because of my bad reputation.

pull through: recover, survive » The dog attacked by the lion is seriously injured. I don't think it will ***pull through***.

put sth down to: attribute to » The parents always ***put*** *their children misbehavior in classroom* ***down to*** some kind of disorder, but not always is this true.

put sb up: offer accommodation » We can ***put you up*** for the night if you need.

put up with: tolerate » I'm telling you once and for all that I will not ***put up with*** your feeble excuses to miss classes.

rule out: exclude » Investigations have already ***ruled out*** a terrorist attack. Instead, they're considering other explanations.

run across: meet by chance » The other day I ***ran across*** an old friend of mine at the airport.

run out of: use up » We're ***running out*** of gas. We'll have to stop at a gas station to fill up.

see into: investigate » I complained to the hotel manager about the service and he said he'd ***see into*** it.

see sb off: accompany to departure » Are you going to ***see*** *your friend* ***off*** at the bust station?

see sb through: help » Don't worry about anything. I'll ***see*** *you* ***through*** during your stay here.

set off: begin a journey » Go to bed early because we'll have to ***set off*** early tomorrow.

set up: institute » They're ***setting up*** a board of examiners to devise the final tests.

settle down:
1. marry » Don't you think you're old enough to ***settle down*** and lead a normal life?
2. establish yourself permanently in a place » When will you ever stop moving places and ***settle down*** in a definitive city?
3. ***settle down to***: apply yourself to » It's time you ***settled down to*** your studies if you want to grab the best opportunities in the future.

show up: appear » We were waiting for Richard to arrive, but he didn't ***show up*** at the party.

sort out: deal with » I hope I'll be able to ***sort out*** all the trouble I have with the embassy.

stand in for: substitute » My teacher couldn't come and she sent someone to ***stand in for*** her today.

stand out: be noticeable » He's a brilliant worker who ***stands out*** from the rest of the group.

stand up for: defend » It's time you learned to ***stand up for*** your rights.

straighten sth out: put right, sort out » I've had some trouble with the embassy, but I've already been able to ***straighten*** *it* ***out***.

take after: look like, resemble in character or appearance » She ***takes after*** her mother in her desire to make the world a better place.

take sb in: fool, trick » You've ***taken*** *me* ***in*** once again with your lies. I won't lend you any money.

take up with: become friends » Even though he was only a freshman, he ***took up with*** the other students from the university easily.

take sb into: persuade by talking » It's no use trying to ***talk*** *me* ***into*** helping you with your schoolwork.

talk sb out: dissuade by talking » I've tried to ***talk*** *my father* ***out*** of smoking, but he won't listen.

tell sb off: reprimand » The boss will ***tell*** *you* ***off*** when he finds out you've forgotten to turn the computer off.

wear off: lose interest » I'm afraid to tell you my enthusiasm for my project ***has*** *already* ***worn off***.

wind down: relax » You'll have a heart attack, Antony. Why don't you move out to the country to ***wind down*** a bit?

EXTRAS I

PHRASAL VERB RELATED NOUNS

Some nouns (and adjectives) are related to a phrasal verb. For example, "set out" becomes "outset", as used in the expression "at the outset" (= "at the beginning"). Take a look at the following nouns and adjectives derived from phrasal verbs (there might be other meanings):

breakdown » failure: "The breakdown of their relationship made them feel so sad."

breakthrough » an important advancement in science: "The discovery of DNA was a major scientific breakthrough."

dropout » someone who leaves school before finishing it, or someone who lives an unconventional life: "He decided he would be a dropout ever since he met those beatnik friends."

getaway » escape (the same as "breakout"): "The robbers made their getaway in a stolen car."

grown-up » adult: "You're already very grown-up to take proper care of your life."

handout » a kind of document: "Please refer to your handouts for information on examination procedures and dates."

layoff » temporary dismissal from job because a company cannot pay workers: "There were massive layoffs in the company due to the crisis."

onset » 1. beginning: "the onset of winter"; 2. attack: "the onset of a disease"

onlooker » spectator "The streets were full of onlookers who gathered to see the accident."

outburst » explosion: "My mother had an outburst of temper when she found out I was pregnant."

outcome » result: "Demonstrators expect the outcome of the protests will be positive."

outlook » attitude towards life: "You should try to change your negative outlook on life."

stopover » short stay in a place in between parts of a journey: "Our flight made an stopover in Paris on our way to Dubai."

takeaway » a shop or restaurant where you buy food to eat somewhere else: "We wanted to find a Chinese takeaway to buy some food."

turnout » the number of people who go to a place or take part in an activity: "There was a massive turnout of people at the company's anniversary party."

upbringing » the things our parents teach us in the process of growing up: "Our personality as adults depends a lot on what our upbringing was like."

uprising » rebellion, revolt: "In Brazil we have witnessed a popular uprising against corruption."

EXTRAS J

DO OR MAKE? (special collocation problems)

There is no rule which guides the correct use of "do" or "make" in some collocation patterns. Therefore, you should practice a lot so you can use these two verbs confidently. Practice using these verbs by choosing the correct answer. Check your answers in the answer key.

	MAKE	DO
example: the bed	✓	
an appointment		
damage		
the dishes		
a decision		
an effort		
someone a favor		
the washing		
research		
an impression		
a noise		
progress		
an exam		
your hair		
karate		
nothing		
a promise		
a suggestion		
your will		
a degree		

ANSWERS TO SECTION 10

	make	do
example: the bed	✓	
an appointment	✓	
damage		✓
the dishes		✓
a decision	✓	
an effort	✓	
someone a favor		✓
the washing		✓
research		✓
an impression	✓	
a noise	✓	
progress	✓	
an exam		✓
your hair		✓
karate		✓
nothing		✓
a promise	✓	
a suggestion	✓	
your will	✓	
a degree		✓

WORD LIST

(The number in parentheses refers to the unit in which the word appears.)

You can use the word list below as a way of reviewing the content from time to time. Just pick out any word and try to see if you can come up with a sentence to illustrate its meaning. If you can't remember exactly what the word means, refer to the unit in which the word appears and check it again for meaning and then write your own example. It might be useful to keep a vocabulary review notebook to do this activity.

abandon (23)
abhor (13)
abrasiveness (12)
abreast (36)
abrogated (37)
absconded (15)
abysmal (45)
acclimatize (16)
accommodating (36)
account for (36)
acerbity (13)
acquaintances (11)
acquiesce (2)
adamant (29)
adroit (47)
affluence (14)
affordable (10)
aghast (41)
airborne (34)
alacrity (21)
allowance (43)
aloof (8)
altruistic (2)
anodyne (12)
answerable (47)
apathetic (18)
aplomb (25)
appalling (17)
appease (1)
appreciably (2)
apprised (41)
apt (25)
arguably (5)
artifice (40)
assertively (10)
asset (37)
assignments (23)
asylum (37)
atmospheric (37)
attainable (27)
austerity (21)
authoritative (24)
averse (13)
avert (46)
avid (35)
avowed (49)
backdrop (25)
backlash (17)
backlog (36)
baffling (9)
baleful (15)
banish (23)
barren (45)
begetting (31)
beguiling (38)
behold (31)
besieged (38)
bewildering (19)
biased (7
bigotry (39)
blackmail (41)
bleak (12)
blithe (42)
blunt (18)
boastful (6)
boisterous (29)
boost (9)
bragging (30)
burden (19)
burgeoning (40)
by all accounts (1)
cajoled (28)
callous (2)
casualties (2)
cauldron (12)
chimerical (50)
clerical (26)
clique (49)
cogently (38)
come up against (14)
comely (40)
commonplace (47)
compelled (3)
compelling (32)
complacency (17)
complacent (11)
complicity (15)
comprehensive (2)
comprised (18)
compromise (44)
conceal (24)
concede (26)
concise (45)
condone (3)
conducive (40)
conscientious (19)
conspicuous (48)
contentious (17)
contingent (50)
convoluted (42)
convoluted (47)
cornerstones (30)
corroborate (11)
counteract (28)
crestfallen (50)
cumbersome (27)
cursory (8)
cut down on (2)
dauntless (15)
dazzling (38)
dearth (19)
debauchery (39)
deceit (11)
deferential (15)
defuse (31)
deleterious (31)
delude (22)
delusional (4)
demean (17)
demeanor (18)
depicts (10)
derelict (20)
derisive (28)
despondent (45)
deterrent (2)
detrimental (5)
devoid (28)
diffident (43)
diligence (30)
discerning (1)
discrepancy (19)
disenfranchised (24)
disheartening (11)
disheveled (13)
dismally (44)
dismissive (27)

REFERENCES

Printed Dictionaries

Longman Dictionary of Contemporary English. The living dictionary. England: Longman, 2003

Collins Cobuild English Dictionary for Advanced Learners: Glasgow: HarperCollins Publishers, 2001

RODALE, J. I. ***The synonym finder***. New York: Warner Books. sem data

On line Free Dictionary

Merriam Webster

Cambridge Online

Oxford Online

Books

HEWINGS, Martin. ***Advanced grammar in use***. 2nd ed. Cambridge: CUP, 2001.

LANDO, Isa Mara. ***Vocabulando***. São Paulo: DISAL, 2006.

SEIDL, J., McMORDIE, W. ***English Idioms and How to Use Them***. Oxford: OUP, 1978.

SWAN, M. ***Practical English Usage***. Oxford: OUP, 2011.

VINCE, M. ***Advanced Language Practice***. Oxford: Macmillan, 2009.

IMPRESSO NA PAYM
EM MAIO DE 2025